A NEW PERSPECTIVE FOR EUROPEAN SPATIAL DEVELOPMENT POLICIES

A New Perspective for European Spatial Development Policies

Edited by
WOLFGANG BLAAS

in cooperation with
EGON MATZNER
LEO VAN DER MEER
GERHARD SCHIMAK
FRIEDRICH SCHINDEGGER

Routledge
Taylor & Francis Group

LONDON AND NEW YORK

First published 1998 by Ashgate Publishing

Reissued 2018 by Routledge
2 Park Square, Milton Park, Abingdon, Oxon OX14 4RN
711 Third Avenue, New York, NY 10017, USA

Routledge is an imprint of the Taylor & Francis Group, an informa business

Publisher's Note
The publisher has gone to great lengths to ensure the quality of this reprint but points out that some imperfections in the original copies may be apparent.

Disclaimer
The publisher has made every effort to trace copyright holders and welcomes correspondence from those they have been unable to contact.

A Library of Congress record exists under LC control number: 97076941

ISBN 13: 978-1-138-60940-2 (hbk)
ISBN 13: 978-0-429-46464-5 (ebk)

Contents

Figures and Tables   vii
Contributors   viii

Foreword: The Vienna Workshop   ix
    Leo Van der Meer

1   Introduction and Summary   **1**
    Wolfgang Blaas

PART I: SCENARIOS

2   Red Octopus   **9**
    Leo Van der Meer
    Discussion by: Peter Schneidewind
3   Euro-Megalopolis or Theme Park Europe?   **27**
    Klaus R. Kunzmann
    Discussion by: Heinz Fassmann

PART II: POLICIES

4   Policies without Inexpert Regulation and Partial Anarchy **59**
    Benny Hjern
    Discussion by: Michael Spindelegger
**5   New Dimensions to Regional Theory and Policy
    in the European Union**   **86**
    Stuart Holland
    Discussion by: Michael Steiner
6   A Plea for Cooperative Strategies for Europe **119**
    Egon Matzner
    Discussion by: Wolf Huber

PART III: EVALUATION

7   Criteria for an Ex Ante Appraisal of Concepts of
     European Spatial Development Policies   135
     Peter Treuner
     Discussion by: Elisabeth Holzinger

PART IV: CONCLUSIONS

8   European Spatial Policies as a Political Requirement   151
     Friedrich Schindegger

INDEX   159

Figures and Tables

Figure 2.1	Red Octopus	13
Figure 2.2	Lacko-Slope	21
Figure 2.3	Lacko-Slope: Scenario 1	21
Figure 2.4	Lacko-Slope: Scenario 2	22
Figure 2.5	European Integration Process	24
Figure 3.1	The spatial structure of the European city region in the 1990s	35
Figure 3.2	The Euro-megalopolis	46
Figure 3.3	Theme Park Europe	47
Figure 3.4	Europe of sustainable regions	49
Figure 3.5	Europe, going East	50
Figure 3.6	Virtual Europe	51
Table 5.1	Traditional and New Regional Policies	88
Table 5.2	Comparision of Frameworks	89
Table 5.3	Allocating a Share of 100 billion ECU EIF on Cohesion Criteria	99
Figure 5.1	Graph of Functional Linkages	109
Figure 5.2	Groups of Industries with Spatial Association	110
Figure 5.3	Graph with Combination of Functional Linkage and Spatial Association	111
Figure 5.4	Cluster	113
Figure 5.5	Technological Cluster	113
Figure 6.1	Transborder cooperation between poor and rich countries	126

Contributors

Blaas Wolfgang	Associate Professor of Economics, Vienna University of Technology, Austria
Fassmann Heinz	Professor of Geography, Technical University München, Germany
Hjern Benny	Professor of Implementation Research, Jönköping International Business School, Sweden
Holland Stuart	Economist, Associate Research in Economy and Society, London, UK
Holzinger Elisabeth	Researcher, Austrian Institute for Regional Studies and Spatial Planning, Vienna, Austria
Huber Wolf	Director, Division for the Coordination of Spatial Planning and Regional Policy, Federal Chancellery, Vienna, Austria
Kunzmann Klaus R.	Professor of Spatial Planning in Europe, University Dortmund, Germany
Matzner Egon	Professor of Public Economics and Infrastucture Policy, Vienna University of Technology, Austria
Schindegger Friedrich	Senior Researcher, Austrian Institute for Regional Studies and Spatial Planning, Vienna, Austria
Schneidewind Peter	Director, Austrian Institute for Regional Studies and Spatial Planning, Vienna, Austria
Spindelegger Michael	Member of the Austrian Parliament
Steiner Michael	Associate Professor of Economics, University of Graz, Austria
Treuner Peter	Professor of Regional Development Planning and Director of the Institute of Regional Development Planning of the University of Stuttgart, Germany
Van der Meer Leo	Van der Meer Associates, Arnhem, The Netherlands

Foreword: The Vienna Workshop

In 1995, a small group of regional planners and social scientists[1] met in Vienna to consider the idea of having an international exchange of views and opinions on spatial development in Europe. Eventually it was decided to organize a workshop in Vienna with the title 'Desiderata for a further development of European Spatial Development Policies', and to invite respected and well-known European experts on this topic.

In January 1996, the event which is called subsequently *The Vienna Workshop* took place with financial and non-financial support of the Research Unit for Socio-Economics of the Austrian Academy of Sciences, and the Austrian Federal Ministry of Science, Research and Art.

The two-day workshop was held in Vienna for two reasons:

1. To promote discussions in Austria, being a new member of the European Union, concerning the elaboration of spatial development strategies and policies of the European Union.
2. To investigate how Austria's knowledge in the field of regional development and 'East-West' relations could be integrated in the European research network.

The aim of the workshop was to enhance knowledge and to exchange views on the issues of present and future spatial development policies in Europe, and to stimulate a discussion on prospective research structures and research topics as a basis for policy development. The workshop was attended by 22 invited experts in the field of European policies with regard to spatial and regional development and regional cooperation.

This book resulting from the workshop may be seen as a modest contribution to laying some foundations for a better understanding of spatial processes, options and policies in Europe. It collects all lectures delivered at
the workshop together with the respective discussant's opinions. Furthermore, there is a summary of all these contributions (in the introductory chapter), and there has been amended a final chapter with conclusions sug-

gested by the spirit and the content of the discussions at *The Vienna Workshop*.

The Austrian Academy of Sciences together with the Federal Ministry of Science, Research and Art express their hope that this workshop publication will trigger off further research in this field and will give rise to further initiatives to structure research and development.

LEO VAN DER MEER
for The Vienna Workshop Group

Note

1 The team consisted of Egon Matzner (Professor of Public Economics and Infrastructure Policy; Vienna University of Technology); Leo van der Meer (Regional Planner; Van der Meer Associates, Arnhem); Friedrich Schindegger (Regional Scientist; Austrian Institute for Regional Studies and Spatial Planning); Gerhard Schimak (Associate Professor of Urban and Regional Planning; Vienna University of Technology) and Wolfgang Blaas (Professor of Economics; Vienna University of Technology).

1 Introduction and Summary

WOLFGANG BLAAS

Introduction

The European Union has no mandate in spatial planning, as this is the responsibility of national, regional, and local authorities in the Union. Nevertheless, EU-policies have a lot of spatial impacts, and the spatial structures are, at the same time, a precondition and the subject matter of various EU-policies.

The imbalance in spatial development in Europe was recently acknowledged and thus spatial policy was put on the political agenda. In 1989 the informal Conference of Ministers responsible for Regional Policy and Spatial Planning was established and followed by the Committee on Spatial Development in 1991.

Also the European Council, European Parliament and the Committee of the Regions expressed the need for an overall coherent picture of the structure of the European territories and the necessity to undertake action in Europe in the fields of spatial cooperation and spatial planning.

The reasons for this need were essentially the following:

1. The development leading to an increasing spatial imbalance in Europe will hinder one of the main (yet often neglected) political goals of the Union: improving social and economic cohesion;[1]
2. Spatially oriented policies can contribute to an economically more competitive Europe and can help to solve congestion problems in Europe's core regions and reverse depopulation in peripheral regions;
3. The trend towards widening and deepening of regional policies;the increase of cross-border and interregional cooperation, initiated by the EU Structure Funds;
4. The spatial consequences of various sector policies in the field of transport (T.E.N. - Trans European Networks), environment, agriculture, etc..

In recognising these facts, the European Commission published in 1991 'Europe 2000' (Outlook for the development of the Communities' Territory) and, three years later, 'Europe 2000+' (Co-operation for European territorial development), in order to enhance a discussion on policy and spatial research issues, and to provide a basis for territorial policy-making.

At the moment the informal 'Conference of Ministers responsible for Regional Policy and Spatial Planning' is preparing a policy document, called 'The European Spatial Development Policy', which was begun in Leipzig (1994) and will be published probably during the Dutch presidency in 1997.

Finally, it should be noted that the mushrooming cross-border co-operation between regions and cities, and particularly between the EU-regions and regions in Central and Eastern Europe, are sources which ask for more knowledge and understanding in the areas of regional science and spatial planning.

Summary of the papers

The papers in this volume look at European spatial development policies from quite different angles. This is as useful and stimulating as it is difficult to sum up. Therefore, in this summary, the original chronological order of presentation at the workshop has been abandoned. The contributions have been regrouped in a way that is suggested by their content and main arguments. We start with scenarios for future spatial developments in Europe, continue with spatial policy considerations and finally take up the question of policy evaluation.

In part I, *Van der Meer* and *Kunzmann* develop a number of European spatial scenarios for the next 20 to 50 years. Whereas Kunzmann discusses five different possible paths of spatial evolution, Van der Meer concentrates on a single scenario, which he calls 'Red Octopus'.

This Red Octopus is a deliberate contrast to the well-known 'Blue Banana', referring to the core areas of economic and industrial development within EU-Europe. Van der Meer argues that it is necessary to counterbalance the growing concentration in the core group of regions by structured deconcentration, e.g. by the creation of new development corridors. This 'octopus-like' branching out of highly developed core areas, may be favoured against the 'banana-outlook' for a number of good reasons. Hence, Van der Meer's deliberations represent a normative scenario including also some policy prescriptions.

In his comment *Schneidewind* proposes deliberations should not be confined to just one objective, namely, socio-economic cohesion at the EU-level. Cohesion at the national and also the regional levels is equally important.

Kunzmann identifies three general spatial trends, namely increasing (1) spatial specialization, (2) spatial differentiation and (3) spatial polarization. These general trends, paralleled by changing value systems and behavioural patterns, produce new spatial categories which, in turn, and together with political and socio-economic developments, give rise to possible patterns of spatial evolution. Kunzmann discusses five different scenarios, which are partly alternative and partly complementary.

The first scenario, 'Euro-megalopolis', emerges from the vision of a further concentration of urban power and activities in Europe, which would lead to a huge, fully urbanized Euro-megalopolis consisting of a few cooperating global command centres, such as Paris, London, Brussels, Frankfurt, with their adjacent urban regions. The second scenario, 'Theme Park Europe' relates to the fact that already now Europe is a much wanted tourist target for Asian tourists, and the outlook for the next century along these lines may imply a particularly important role for conservation and modernization policies in Europe. A 'Europe of sustainable regions'. The third scenario, a 'Europe of sustainable regions', envisages a deliberate policy of cutting back unnecessary mobility, the support of endogeneous regional potentials, and a regional specialization in order to survive in the global market. In his fourth scenario, 'Europe, Going East?', Kunzmann argues that the development of a corridor of Central and Eastern European city regions reaching from Warsaw over Wroclaw to Prague and Budapest seems likely, with Berlin, Dresden, Nuremberg and Vienna as exchange nodes between East and West. Finally, Europe's spatial future may look quite different from now when the decentralization potential of the new information technologies are being fully utilized within the next generations. In a 'Virtual Europe', larger European cities may be surrounded by information belts, and traditional holiday regions in Europe may become transformed into permanent or semi-permanent multi-cultural residential communities.

The value of Kunzmann's paper, as seen by *Faßmann*, results primarily from the fact that the scenarios offer an interesting starting point for further discussion, though they are extreme and will never become realities.

In part II, Hjern, Holland and Matzner deal with policy.

Hjern makes a case for a spatial development policy which is structured to make local governments increasingly accountable for a small number of programmes. These programmes should be mainly concerned with technological qualification strategies, leaving aside spatially redistributive aims.

In his comment on Hjern, *Spindelegger* advocates a more differentiated view on centralism vs. decentralization. He reminds us of the limits of cecentralized, independent actions of regions.

Holland's contribution takes micro-economic policy as its perspective. He makes some suggestions how regional policies could be employed to support small and medium-sized firms. The idea is that through interregional cooperation ('networking') successful smaller firms could gain some of the strengths of multinational firms without themselves becoming large multinationals. The paper then analyzes some of the EU-programmes and their effects on fostering the networking of small and medium firms.

Steiner agrees in his comment that most new ideas and projects have arisen out of intensive personal cooperation and informal contacts. However, he raises doubts whether forming complexes by means of cooperation and alliances were a decisive entrepreneurial strategy, since firms have little interest and intention to cooperate.

To enhance this interest to cooperate - not only of firms, but more generally of economic and political decision-makers - is seen as an overriding objective by *Matzner*. He uses game theoretic metaphors to show the importance of the socio-economic context for the outcome of interdependent economic and political decisions. It is suggested that institutional contexts could be changed in such a way that negative sum games become less likely and positive sum games become more likely.

Huber, in his comment on Matzner, reminds us that political life is much more complex than game theoretic models may suggest, and that it is in general very costly to reduce complexity and uncertainty to a level which allows something near rational decision making. Therefore, at least in many cases of practical decision making, a kind of 'bounded rationality approach' to cooperation will be observed. For example, urgent decisions have to be taken without knowing all the possible decision effects; or it may be possible to cooperate only implicitly by considering in advance also the interests of other players without any explicit negotiation, etc.

The question on how to evaluate different variants of spatial policy programmes is taken up by *Treuner* in part III. He develops seven criteria which are regarded as fundamental for the appraisal of European spatial development policies: (1) ability to respond to European (i.e. non-national) priorities; (2) respect for the principle of subsidiarity; (3) analytical foundation; (4) balance between efficiency and integration; (5) balance between short-term and long-term development objectives; (6) programme character of policies (complementary nature of actions etc.) and (7) partnership approach.

As an example, Treuner goes through these criteria applied to the European Regional Development Fund. This programme is chosen as the most interesting being an explicitly space-oriented programme of the EU, but it is shown to be unsatisfactory for most of the suggested criteria.

Finally, in part IV some conclusions are drawn by *Schindegger* concerning meaningful policy reactions to the challenges ahead. In particular it is postulated, that cohesion is the grand objective not only at the European, but also at the national level. In order to reach this goal, EU's regional policy, among other things, has to be shaped with the participation of the cities as regional centres. To work out and supply the scientific foundations for these policies, it may eventually turn out to be quite useful to develop an EU research centre for spatial development in Central and Eastern Europe.

Note

1   See Ash Amin and John Tomaney (1995), The Regional Dilemma in a Neo-Liberal Europe. In: European Urban and Regional Studies 2, No. 2, 171-188.

PART I: SCENARIOS

2 Red Octopus

LEO VAN DER MEER

A European Spatial Scenario

It was a pleasure to take part in the preparation for this workshop and to contribute to the workshop-paper called 'Desiderata for a further development of European Spatial Development Policies'. However, as a policy-adviser I feel - before an academic audience and in the setting of the Austrian Academy of Sciences - a bit awkward in presenting you a policy-oriented draft of a European Spatial Scenario called 'Red Octopus', which might give you the idea of a James Bond, or even Mafia-like, approach.

In my scenario, which is still in the stage of conception and not yet very well explored, I would like to take you to the year 2046 and show you the virtual reality of that time, as one of the many options and visions.

Research into, and the development of, policy-oriented scenarios might help to obtain a better understanding of spatial processes that would emerge and, in this way, possibly might provide guiding principles for private and public short-term decision-making. This sounds rather optimistic since we have at the moment no authority which can decide over spatial planning issues that go beyond the national boundaries. The European Union has no mandate in the field and the Member States are, so far, reluctant to produce the 'European Spatial Development Perspective' (E.S.D.P.) as a political planning document.

Nevertheless, I think that scenarios are very good as a tool which forces one to think about the future and to help to make good decisions in the present with medium and long-term policies in view.

In my lecture I will first describe some insights and recent policies at the European level, followed by the Red Octopus Scenario and assumptions concerning processes in the coming fifty years, and finally I will draw some conclusions.

European Spatial Planning Now

The Maastricht Treaty and the Delors White Paper share one of the most important political aims of the European Union, namely, social and economic cohesion throughout Europe and therefore a better and more just balance between the regions. Regional disparities should be narrowed, solidarity between regions and social groups should emerge, policies should be geared towards sustainable developments and at the same time Europe's economy should be made more competitive vis-à-vis the United States and Japan. A more effective cooperation between Commission, Member States and regional authorities will be necessary to achieve these goals.

It is rather obvious that spatial organization is at stake when talking about these issues. The spatial factor will become even more relevant since the Union faces new challenges in Eastern Europe. Former USSR-satellites are knocking at the EU door. Eastern European countries will become important economic partners and their entry in the Union will become necessary in terms of the same policy towards a better balance between the regions in Europe and because of safety and keeping the peace in Europe.

Finally, Maastricht adapted the development of Trans-European Networks as a contribution to social and economic cohesion, by arguing that it is necessary to link island, landlocked and peripheral regions with the central regions of the Community.

Also a policy that influences the spatial organization.

Spatial Development itself recently became a subject of the European Commission. Background thinking: if we leave the spatial organization as it is, we will witness more disparities between the 'rich' and the 'poor' regions, or the 'centre' and the 'periphery', and a less competitive Europe due to congestion and overheating in the 'centre'.

The Commission has launched already two main policy documents:

1. Europe 2000 (1991) - Outlook for the Development of the Community's Territory, and
2. Europe 2000+ (1994) - Cooperation for European Territorial Development.

On the way to a more balanced development of the Community and discovering that the instrument of the Structure Funds alone did not lead towards more cohesion and balance between periphery and the centre, Europe 2000 was produced by the Commission and accepted by the Council. It provided a significant advance in understanding the factors shaping the organization of European territory, and showed that there is a need for more cooperation and active involvement of the Union States and Member States collectively in spatial organization matters.

Exactly this very need became the subtitle of *Europe 2000+*: coop-eration at the political level (instead of outlook for planners), aiming at long-term policies.

I will just list from various sources some trends and events which favour and even ask for medium and long-term visionary spatial development strategies:

1. Interdependency between regions in Europe is acknowledged, and co-operation between regions in spatial development is booming (INTERREG I and II);
2. The informal Minister Conference on spatial planning created a Committee on Spatial Development, which is on its way to propose a European Spatial Development Perspective (E.S.P.D.);
3. Member States, the Council of Europe, OESO, and the Committee of the Regions are more and more convinced that a vision on the development of European space is a necessity;
4. Migration and brain-drain from periphery towards centre leaving large areas depopulated and no longer capable of using endogenous potentials;
5. The entry of the former East German provinces and Austria combined with the opening of Eastern Europe, as new markets and growing economies (having the advantage of low labour costs and high level of professional and scientific education), will introduce an East-West dimension in Europe next to the traditional North-South dimension;
6. The overall concerns about our natural environment, which is endangered all over the Continent in various ways, needs to be considered in connection with urbanization and transport across Europe.

As a basis for my scenario, I will use the following points of departure as condensed from the above mentioned views:

1. In order to achieve more socio-economic cohesion and an economically more competitive Europe, an increase in balance between 'centre' and 'periphery' is necessary. Spatial organization can play a role in achieving these political goals.
2. Endogenous potentials are to be nurtured in order to develop regions outside the European core.

3. Spatial initiatives should be developed to provide alternative growth poles and zones in order to achieve more cohesion and more balance, as well as to diminish congestion and scarcity of land in the urban core area.
4. New markets, new options, new networks should be conceived as options to strengthen the East-West dimension next to the North-South.
5. Cross-border cooperation in the field of spatial organization will intensify according to the already existing trends (supported by the EU Funds).
6. Trans-European Networks will be necessary and considered as triggers of economic progress.
7. Growing political and economic influence of regions in Europe which will intensify direct relations with the European Commission (the so-called regionalization in Europe).

Long before the E.S.D.P. is to be accepted and published (probably during the Dutch presidency in 1997), in which many of the above mentioned issues will be dealt with, I would now like to present my scenario to you.

RED OCTOPUS: A European Spatial Cohesion Scenario

Today, on January 26th in the year 2046, we are attending a two-day conference organized by the European Academy of Sciences and are listening to the keynote speaker, Her Excellency the Minister of Spatial Planning, member of the cabinet of the Federal European State (FES). Her topic is 'European Spatial Planning: Past and Present'.

I will give you an abstract of her most interesting speech.

Europe's spatial organization has changed dramatically as compared with the nineties of the former century, as that decade marked the end of a century of political chaos, growing discrepancies and disparities between the central regions and more peripheral regions, and also post-Communist uncertainties. As a matter of fact, the Treaty of Maastricht (Socio-Economic Cohesion, Monetary Union, and Single Market), at that time not very well received, and the fall of the Iron Curtain, became the turning points leading to new spatial initiatives, extension of the Union with former Eastern European countries (2000-2015) and finally, ten years ago, the erection of the Federal European State.

Policies towards a safer and economically and socially more balanced Europe are well on their way to settling down structurally, and, at the same time, the environmental condition of Europe has improved. Europe's prime Central Urban Core Area (once named 'Blue Banana'), still the 'corpus major' of the economy, science and technology, and main source of innovation, is now a part of an integrated larger system of body and arms reaching into Northern, Eastern and Southern parts of Europe. The arms are in fact longitudinal corridors composed of regions and cities directly linked with the traditional main-centres of business and innovations. I would like to call this whole dynamic spatio-economical system 'The Red Octopus' (a more lively concept than the static 'Blue Banana').

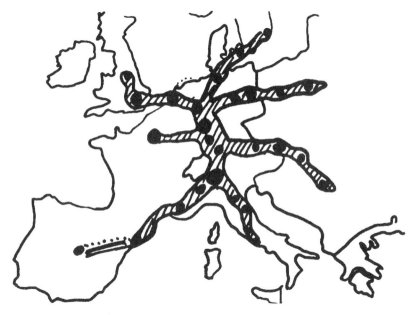

Figure 2.1 Red Octopus

Source: Based on Author's own draft

The new corridors of urbanization are developing rapidly and are supported by the Trans-European Network, the European Macro-Ecological Structure, and a strong inter-regional cooperation. In the Red Octopus, the number of islands of innovation (Archipelago) have almost doubled as compared with 50 years ago. New islands of innovation, connected with strings of intermediate, medium-sized trade and industrial centres to the ten traditional islands, are Copenhagen, Berlin, Warsaw, Vienna, Belgrade, Budapest, Rome, Barcelona and Madrid. Examples of intermediate agglomerations/regions which are specialized in distinctive economic and innovative sectors are, for instance, Hamburg,

Braunschweig-Göttingen, Poznan, Salzburg-Linz, Florence, Marseille, and Lyon-Grenoble.

The *Red Octopus*, as an urbanized system, is supported by the Macro-Ecological Structure (M.E.S.), an interlinked system of regions that safeguards natural habitats of flora and fauna and a natural (full or part-time) environment for human beings. The M.E.S. provides for large storage facilities for (drinking) water, restores and extends the forest areas, and provides agricultural products for regional markets. The economy in these rural regions is based on endogenous potentials making use of amenities which are scarce in the *Red Octopus* system: open air, natural and cultural heritage, and sustainable forms of recreation.specialized small- and medium-sized firms provide for most of the employment.

These regions are functioning in interregional networks determined either by common interests (economic similarities, tourism, environment) or by geographical location/characteristics. For example: wine regions, fishing ports, coastal regions, alpine regions, lake regions. In general the regional authorities and regional organizations are the engines of economic development.

The difference both in the GDPs per capita of the European countries and, likewise, the difference between the GRP per capita of the European regions has diminished, thanks to macro-European spatio-economic planning policies framed in the *Red Octopus* concept. The economic growth in more peripheral regions, which now have much better accessibility to the European Core Area and are better connected with surrounding regional capitals, is steady.

The Minister went on with listing the *most important factors* in the past fifty years, that were responsible for the dramatical change in spatial organization called *Red Octopus*:

1. Eastern European countries became members of the FES. Their fast growing economies, thanks to competitive building-material and labour costs, their traditionally high level of university-educated labour force, and their large city economies, produced a number of innovative and knowledge-based cities, which became important technological growth poles.

2. Trade, communication and transport systems shifted from a pure North-South dimension to a combined East-West and North-South dimension.

3. East-West corridors developed as a consequence of the deconcentration tendencies from *the Blue Banana* as well as cohesion policies from the FES (objective I status) and the regional authorities, who wanted to im-

prove accessibility and to become connected with the European core system *Red Octopus*.

4. European multinationals started to invest increasingly, from 2005 onwards, in manufacturing, research and computerised administrative services in Eastern Europe because
   a) Compared with West European cities, it proved to be more profitable,
   b) Profitability of investing in South-East Asia has gone down (transport costs, adverse regimes),
   c) Subsidies from FES (structure funds and tax facilities.
   d) Already back in 1996, the Brady-bonds in Poland were promoted to 'investment   grade' and EBRD bonds became linked to the zloty currency.
   e) Also in the 'nineties, European investment streams shifted to China and Eastern Europe as compared with the 'seventies (Singapore, Taiwan, Hongkong) and the 'eighties (Indonesia, Mexico, Malaysia).

5. The FES, national and regional policies to restore natural habitats, and to safeguard water, woods and soil, gave rise to the creation of the macro-ecological structure consisting of vast open areas between the high density urbanized *Octopus* arms.
   Along with agricultural and touristic assets, successful regions emerged. For example: the Mazurian Lake District, Bavarian-Bohemian Forest, Pyrenees, Frisian Lake and Coast District, Ardennes-Eifel Region, etc..

6. The FES policy, which started in 1998 with the European Spatial Development Perspective, towards the concentration of science, technology, innovation, tertiary economy, and therefore population, in the main corridors stretching to Northern, Eastern and Southern parts of Europe (Octopus), became a success because it was supported by major private players: the European Board of Large Industries, the Union of Large Cities (formerly Eurocities), the European Railway Association, the European Environmental Institute, and the Committee of the Regions.

7. The understanding (deepened by the Bosnian War) to make Europe more safe by means of a more balanced growth.

As for the East-West dimension, two Red Octopus arms are quite successful:

1. Amsterdam/Rotterdam - Ruhr Area - Braunschweig/Göttingen - Berlin - Poznan - Warsaw.

2. Stuttgart - Ulm - Munich - Salzburg/Linz - Vienna - Budapest - Belgrade.

Each arm consists of a network of cities and city regions benefiting from mutual cooperation, specialization, and the exchange of knowledge and information (Triangulation, Transregional Cooperation Networks).
Each arm includes:

1. Advanced city regions: islands of innovation and surrounding urbanized areas;
2. Adaptive, intermediate city regions: highly developed city regions well connected with the islands of innovation and specialized in economic functions: trade, manufacturing, education, etc.;
3. Dependent in-between regions: medium and small-sized cities in semirural, regional settings characterized by specialized agriculture, medium-sized industry and professional services in specialized fields (telecommunication-oriented, high-tech on a small scale);
4. A high-density, high-capacity linear system of air, road, rail and telecomunication infrastructures connecting the arm-parts with each other, and the arms to the body of the *Octopus*.

It was rather interesting to notice that, already in the nineties, the parts of the arm were developing thanks to cross-border cooperation between regions, deconcentration of work and people from the large cities, and the development of cross-border inter-regional spatial plans (Poznan became closely linked with the Berlin-region, Salzburg became part of the Munich-region, the Dutch changed their Randstad doctrine to a more West-East oriented system linking the 'Randstad' (a rim city consisting of Amsterdam, Rotterdam, The Hague and Utrecht) with Germany) while new East-West passengers and cargo connections were introduced.

These were the main outlines of her speech concerning past and present European spatial processes.

Before giving the floor to the next speaker, the Minister gave us the latest news on the referendum in Argau. We were not surprised to be informed that the Canton will vote against Swiss FES-membership.

Conclusions

What I have tried to convey to you this afternoon (we are now back in 1996) was not to advocate blueprints or a masterplan for Europe's future spatial organization. I just wanted to share with you some views concerning options for long-term spatial policies.

In this respect, my main points are:

1. The European Commission, Member States (notably Germany and Holland), the Committee of the Regions, and research groups (Hingel, Kuklinski, Rider, etc.) accept the importance of the geographical dimension of socio-economic cohesion and environmental policies. Elaborating, long-term views on the organization of European Space are gaining political momentum and relevance.

2. The development of different, scientifically-based spatial scenarios could be helpful in assessing future spatial developments and in the making of European spatial policies. The creation of a Centre for European Spatial Studies could be an interesting idea.
   (Tasks: - monitoring spatial development
                  - research
                  - spatial scenarios)

3. In order to promote a more balanced Europe and enhanced socio-economic cohesion, to safeguard the European Environment, and to offer growth potentials for peripheral regions, it will be necessary to counter-balance the growing concentration in the core-group of regions (the ten islands of innovation).

4. Counterbalance forces to be used:
   -congestion, prices, scarcity of space in the core,
   -economic growth potentials in Eastern Europe,
   -European money predominantly going to Objective I and Objective II areas,
   -European RTD programmes,
   -creation of new islands of innovation,
   -inter-regional cooperation and networking.

5. The scenario I am proposing is to 'concentrate deconcentration'. Instead of a random dispersion, the creation of new development corridors, stemming from the core, which are putting into line already existing large capital city regions and already emerging linear development.
   A new European-wide core area will emerge, supported by the Trans-European Network, making Europe more competitive, giving better options and accessibility to peripheral regions (cohesion) and leaving ample space for environmental revival.

In short - *Red Octopus.*

6. The implementation of long-term spatial policies (visionary spatial development models, like the *Red Octopus* scenario presented above) depends to a great degree on spatial policy as an instrument of the European Government, as well as congruency between governmental and private sector policies.

I am fully aware that *The Red Octopus* scenario, as one of the many options, is just a first attempt, leaving many questions open. However, I hope to bring this little seed a bit further in the coming future. Maybe we have here a seed that could grow with the help of one of the Commission's programmes.

References

Akademie für Raumforschung und Landesplanung (1995), Tremmer P. und Foucher M.: Towards a New European Space, Hannover.

Committee on Spatial Development (1994): Principles for a European Spatial Development Policy, Leipzig.

Council of the European Union (1992): Verdrag betreffende de Europese Unie (Treaty of Maastricht), Brussels.

Dutch Physical Planning Agency (1991): European Perspectives, The Hague.

European Commission (1991): Europe 2000, Brussels.

European Commission (1991): Europe 2000+, Brussels.

European Commission (1993): Growth, Competitiveness and Employment (White Paper Delors), Brussels.

European Commission (1994): Fifth Periodic Report 'Competition and Cohesion', Brussels.

Eurostat(1995): Statistical Yearbook 1994, Brussels.

European Institute for Regional and Local Development (1994): Baltic Europe in the Perspective of Global Change, Warsaw.

Fast-programme (E.C.) Hingel (1992/1993): Science, Technology and Social and Economic Cohesion - Overall Synthesis, Brussels.

Fast-programme (E.C.) FERE Consultants (1995): Scenario's de politiques communautaires de cohésion et de codévelopment dans une Europe enlargie, Brussels.

Fast-programme (E.C.) Hilpert (1995): Europe's InnovativeCentre - It`s Role for Continental Europe and Community Cohesion, Brussels.

Fast-programme (E.C.) Rider (1995): Regional Transnational Networks of Cooperation in the Fields of Science, Technology, Education and Vocational Training, Brussels.

Gorzelak et al(1994): Eastern and Central Europe 2000, Warsaw.

Institut für Landes- und Stadtentwicklungsforschung (1984): European Regional/Spatial Planning Charter, Dortmund.

Kommission der Europäische Gemeinschaft, Inter G. (1995): Perspektivstudie über die Regionen des Alpenbogen und Alpenrandbereich, Brussels.

Kuklinski A. (1991): Pan-European Spatial Development Policy (PESDIP), Warsaw, 1994.

Kunzmann K. und Wegener M.: The Pattern of Urbanisation 1960-1990, IRPUD, Dortmund.

Maggi-Masser-Nijkamp: Missing Networks (1993): The Case of European Freight Transport, European Planning Studies, Vol. 1, No. 3.

Ministry of Housing (1991): Physical Planning and Environment: Fourth Note (EXTRA) on Physical Planning, The Hague.

N.E.A. (1992): Nieuwe Oost-West gerichter corridors, Rijswijk (NL).

Nijkamp, Vleugel (1993): Success Factors for High Speed Rail Networks in Europe, Int. Journal of Transport Economics, Vol. XX, No. 3, October.

Raad van Advies voor de Ruimtelijke Ordening (1995): Europese Ruimtelijke. Ordening, The Hague.

Discussion by: Peter Schneidewind

On reading Van der Meer's paper, I felt I could not come up with different images of the future, and so I shall do no more than ask some questions. Questions, to which answers may not be available yet, but questions which - it seems to me - have not been asked often or insistently enough. Maybe these questions can contribute to a better understanding of the scope and the functioning of spatial development at the European level.

Van der Meer uses a technique in his scenario which one could label as a 'long term prognosis', conjuring up a picture of spatial structures of a future far enough away to make it legitimate not to look at the processes and activities that lead to these structures. We all know that in the very long run anything seems possible. In the long run all our wishes may come true. A long term prognosis, like the one just presented, therefore tends to reflect the normative objectives that underlie the scenario more than the forces advancing the spatial development process. This is a useful exercise if it serves to open up the discussion about these objectives, which includes making them explicit.

In the scenario presented, and also in the majority of work on spatial development, only one main objective is stated explicitly, namely socio-economic cohesion (of the Union).

This leads to my first question: Does cohesion on the EU level suffice to provide a normative framework for spatial development analysis? Or else, does spatial development ask for more than a single objective?
I would like to put forward two considerations in favour of some additional spatial development objectives.

Let me first take the example of the eastern border of the Union. At a similar workshop to today's, held in the European Council here in Vienna two years ago, Matzner gave a short summary of the situation at that border and the political implications. He nick-named the graphical presentation 'Lacko-slope'.

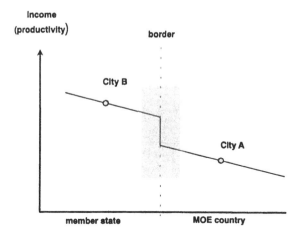

Figure 2.2 Lacko-Slope

Source: Author's own draft, based on Matzner in this volume

This Lacko-slope shows the difference in the national levels of income (and productivity) taking into account a rough approximation of the inequality of these levels within the bordering States. The cohesion objective was easily turned into a desirable scenario which allowed two curves to move parallel to each other but at differnt speeds. Like this:

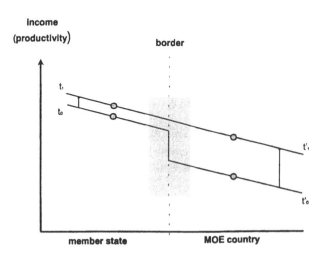

Figure 2.3 Lacko-Slope: Scenario 1

Source: Author's own draft, based on Matzner in this volume

But this is not what happens in fact. Empirical evidence has grown considerably and shows that the two national slopes move in quite different ways. The slope within the reform country does move upwards, but the more it does so, the more it becomes tilted. The inequalities in income are growing considerably and seem to be growing further. On the other hand, the curve in the countries of the single market seem to become slightly more horizontal; at least as far as the Austrian case is concerned. (Similar cases are to be found within some of the Objective-1 countries, such as Portugal and, possibly, also Ireland).

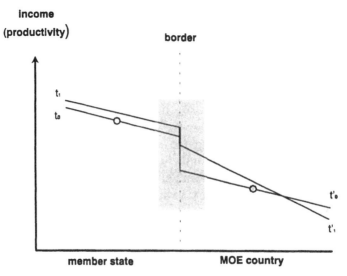

Figure 2.4 Lacko-Slope: Scenario 2

Source: Author's own draft, based on Matzner in this volume

As far as European spatial structure is concerned, this situation may still be in line with the cohesion-objective since the differences, both of the averages and between the neighbouring regions become smaller (even if only at a slow pace).

Furthermore, this growing inequality in the poorer countries may be functional as far as national development policy is concerned.

The other consideration deals with the notion of cohesion itself. I assert that not spatial cohesion, i.e. the imbalances between the regions, is a major topic in the Union, but that social cohesion within the regions or cities is the much more imminent problem. Certainly, in many cases, social cohesion has spatial aspects, but this does not justify taking one for the other. Spatial development policy, in any conceivable sense of the word, does need objectives defined in spatial terms. Otherwise one runs the risk (not only when designing future spatial structures) of doing someone else's job. These spatial objectives may not be conceived as the ultimate distribution of infrastructure and activities, but ought to take the form of (spatial) standards which have to relate to people's needs.

The best example in this respect, I think, is the discussion of the Trans-European Networks (TENs) among spatial analysts. As long as one takes for granted that the TENs foster, in some way or other, spatial cohesion, one cannot contribute genuinely to the debate on their impact and, still less, on their layout. Only spatial criteria and development objectives can provide a basis for a contribution by spatial planners for a more comprehensive view of the TENs, instead of merely reacting to sector policies by making the best out of them.

Second question: Can one still maintain the seemingly obvious affinity of regions (legal or administrative units) and spaces? Since the Treaty of Maastricht it seems to me that these two concepts tend to differ even more.

EU regionalization is becoming increasingly a political concept aimed at the redistribution of legitimate powers between the Union, the Member States and existing regions (of very different kinds). The recent row over the representation of the Tyrolean region illustrates this struggle in Brussels quite impressively.

Spatial development, on the other hand, has to be defined as a spatially relevant socio-economic process, sometimes more or less co-shaped by natural conditions. This does not allow for fixed spatial entities, be they States or regions. These entities have to be defined on a strictly functional basis and therefore have to have varying shapes corresponding to the function(s) under consideration.

Therefore, there is the growing doubt that regionalization, i.e. regional policy, can form the territorial basis of spatial development considerations any longer. Nor can regional policy be considered o play a decisive role in the spatial development process at all; neither at present nor, if one goes by national experience, in the future. It is just another policy sector.

Since spatial development is mainly shaped by sector trends, any analysis has to focus on topics such as technology, transport, agriculture, social changes etc., and the spatial impact of changes in these fields, as well as the spatial impact of the sector policies concerned. Unfortunately, this view does not seem to be shared by those designing future spatial structures as a result of development policy - and who are to be found both within policy-making bodies and in the academic world.

I would like to conclude my contribution by suggesting a very rough and preliminary framework in which spatial development scenarios may be fitted in and which would, at the same time, be suitable to further deepen the discussion on objectives in spatial development.

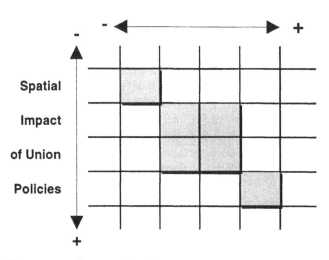

Figure 2.5 European Integration Process

Source: Author's own draft

It takes the common form of two axes; one representing the European integration process and the other representing the impact of sector Union policies - one of which, obviously, would be the Structural Funds policy.

The political integration process would have to take into account not only the enlargement of the Union, but also the deepening process, i.e. the evolvment of new Union policies, especially the monetary union, but maybe also security questions and even institutional reform. We all know that there is a very wide range of political options still open. Nevertheless, it should be possible to categorize this wide range into sets that can be depicted as representing more or less integration.

A similar, but maybe even more tricky categorization, should be achievable for the complex of spatial impacts of sector policies. At the one end of this classification one could imagine the present spatial impacts, respectively their extrapolation into the future, which could be characterized as 'homogenizing'. At the other end of this classification one might put spatial impacts of a kind that represent a greater degree of sustainability of development, possibly on a regional (or even smaller spatial) scale.

   With some analytical skill and wit, one can then take a look at the spatial structure of Europe through emerging 'windows to the future' - as I choose to call the more interesting fields of the grid.

   A framework like this would serve not only as a prognostic tool. It could, in the course of the discussion, lead to the recognition of the spatial impacts of Union policy by people other than those concerned with spatial development. This recognition is the prerequisite for consideration within sector policies, and may finally lead to a redefinition of sector policies. What other aim can spatial development scenario-writing have than this?

3 Euro-Megalopolis or Theme Park Europe?

KLAUS R. KUNZMANN [1]

Scenarios for European Spatial Development

There are three published and widely disseminated key documents that contain elements of European spatial policies- the documents *Europe 2000* and *Europe 2000+* and the Periodical Reports, which monitor at regular intervals selected spatial development trends. All these documents have been commissioned by the European Commission during 1990 to 1994 (COM, 1991, 1994). There are in addition, documents commissioned and published in the 1970s by the Council of Europe that have paved the way for the above activities (e.g. CoE, 1983). Today, however, these documents are just of historical value. Finally, there is a growing number of national (mainly German, French and Dutch and Scandinavian) documents (ARL/DATAR, 1992; BFLR, 1995) which aim at contributing national perspectives to a European spatial development concept, a concept which is, at present, under discussion. One of these documents, presented by the French Presidency on the occasion of the 1995 Strasbourg meeting of the Ministers responsible for spatial planning, contains three trend scenarios for European spatial development (European urban system, European transport network and European natural heritage).

Still the most comprehensive and up-to date document about spatial development trends in Europe is the document *Europe 2000+*. It suggests areas of transitional cooperation (Centre Capital Region, Alpine Arc, Baltic Region etc.), broad factors in regional organization (trans-European networks, regional planning and public transfer systems), developments in rural, urban and border areas, and principles and proposals for joint transnational action and cooperation.

Also a network of European observatories, monitoring spatial development change in Europe, has been suggested in this document.

Starting from this document the Council of Ministers responsible for spatial planning in Europe, on the occasion of its meeting in Barcelona in late 1995, expressed its sincere commitment to the joint development of a spatial development strategy for the territory of the European Union linked to the Structural Funds of the European Commission. It is envisaged that a draft of the European Spatial Development Concept will be presented in 1997 when the Dutch government holds the Presidency of the European Union.

Quite obviously, the resulting concept will not be a blueprint for the shaping and construction of a new Europe. It cannot be compared with plans for buildings or machines. Who should be the contractor, who the overall spatial manager? Nobody would really accept such a value-driven, normative, top-down approach.

Most people in Europe would not even know that such a document is in production. And, frankly, few people would care whether it exists or not. The few, who are aware of the respective activities at the European level, and who know of the efforts to formulate spatial development policies for Europe, are more than sceptical as to the relevance and usefulness of such exercises. In times of global deregulation fever, there is little trust in public policies which aim at influencing spatial development in Europe on a macro-scale. Hence, at first sight, such efforts may indeed be considered to be mere academic rhetoric and more like 'paper tigers' than effective efforts to guide or determine the use of land and resources at a European macro-scale. There is much truth in the critical stance to such cartographic exercises of spatial experts, who mould their analytic findings together with their normative value systems into oversimplified spatial configurations and images such as bananas, grapes, chains, belts or whatever the geographers' and planners' geodesign supermarket offers at low production costs (Brunet, 1989; Kunzmann, 1993a). However, such criticism is too simple. There is some value in such exercises which may justify the efforts.

First, it is widely acknowledged among planning scholars that the process of considering a plan is much more important than the plan itself, which is only the visible final end-product of the planning process. The ongoing process of 15 national institutions cooperating in the production of maps which show spatial development trends by using comparable criteria and cartographic symbols is, *per se,* already sensational. It is undoubtedly a big step forward to a joint cross-cultural understanding of spatial development processes in Europe. The lengthy communication processes which are required to agree on joint criteria and cartographic symbols will develop their own moment.

Second, the visualization of spatial problems in maps makes it much easier to communicate the problems to the public and the political arena. It facilitates the understanding of complex spatial systems, and it reveals the lack of comparable information in Europe.

Third, recent research in Europe has shown that symbols and spatial images play an underestimated role in spatial planning. In the end visualized concepts will contribute more to achieving certain political goals than legal and financial instruments. Visualized spatial symbols, for all their vagueness, can reduce complexity enormously. They are easy to communicate and much easier to grasp and to accept.

Fourth, experience shows that the shortcomings or dissatisfaction with such concepts trigger off new research. Reference to such documents is made when research funds are made available to improve the knowledge of spatial development and interrelationships. The European dimension of the document is a new challenge to spatial research in Europe.

This paper does not aim at developing a consistent concept for European spatial development policy. Its purpose is rather to present some spatial development trends in Europe at the turn of the millennium, to discuss some factors which may influence future spatial development in European cities and regions, and to sketch a few scenario plots for possible spatial futures of the Continent.

General Trends of Spatial Development in Europe at the Turn of the Millennium

Three clear trends determine spatial development in Europe: an increasing spatial specialization, the subsequent spatial differentiation and a growing spatial polarization. These three trends can be observed at all levels of decision-making: the European, the national and the regional levels. For many reasons, though mainly due to faster information and transportation flows, cities and regions are becoming functionally specialized. Quite understandably they focus their economic and political activities on the promotion of local potential such as a traditional economic or agricultural base (unless it is a structurally weak one), on a favourable geopolitical location, on a positive global image, attracting businesses and visitors, on functional advantages such as a logistics or financial centre. In order to strengthen and to modernize the given potential, cities and regions encourage the addition of missing links (e.g. specialized producer-oriented services), the establishment of specialized research and training institutions, or the expansion of logistical facilities. They promote hard and soft location factors necessary to be competitive in a global market. They try to improve their accessibility and infrastructure standards, they fight to attract international and national institutions and enterprises complementing the respective complex, they initiate flagship projects to show initiative and to improve the visual quality of the city and, finally, they sponsor events to attract visitors, to demonstrate their commitment to culture, and to serve a qualified local and regional labour force.

The result is specialized spatial/territorial complexes, where a particular specialization (the automobile industries, cultural industries, aerospace industries) is dominating regional development activities and policies. These regional complexes are dominated by close networks of persons, of actors, of political players, who formulate development goals and regional decision-making processes. Such networks can be open and innovative and future-oriented (Silicon Valley, Orange County and Sophia Antipolis/Nice are famous examples), and they can be closed and defensive, defending a declining regional economic base. Consequently, global specialization is causing intraregional spatial differentiation. This in turn requires a larger territory to accommodate the various requirements of actors playing in the global economy. Hence, global specialization and intraregional differentiation leads unavoidably to a further growth of the urban region in Europe, by expanding more and more into a wider hinterland.

Frankfurt is considered by all to be a rather important European, if not global, city in the centre of western Germany. However, those living and working in the region know that the city of Frankfurt is only the inner core of an urban region which extends to Giessen in the east, Darmstadt in the south, Mainz in the west and Limburg in the north. This is reflected by daily commuter flows to the central city, by the targets of lost luggage delivery services, or by the catchment area of the airport's business or charter passengers . Frankfurt is not a unique case. This is also true for Manchester and Glasgow as for Lyon, Milan, Zurich or Rotterdam, and for other city regions in the champion league of EUROCITIES. The gradual expansion of the city region to a wider hinterland is a European-wide phenomenon. Only recently the German cities of Munich, Augsburg and Ingolstadt decided to respond to speculative development pressure hitting Munich, by forming a strategic alliance called MAI which aims at initiating a certain division of labour between the three cities while strengthening the urban region as a whole.

The development trends sketched above are, and this is agreed knowledge, paralleled by changing value systems and behavioural patterns of the Western society, and additionally driven by more and more privatized or corporate decision-making systems into deregulated politico-administrative milieux. Such development trends bring about a growing spatial differentiation of urban and regional functions and land uses within regions. The scaling up of functions to adapt a city region to global or at least to international standards leads to growing intraregional specialization of single territorial units. While old categories in land use or regional physical plans are obsolete, the emergence of new spatial categories can be observed (Ache et. al., 1991; Kunzmann, 1993b). Such spatial categories are:

International finance and service centres: These are those inner urban quarters of larger city regions in Europe where a great variety of institutions of international finances and services, their forward and backward linkages (media, printing, travel agencies etc.) and the related life spaces of their respective labour force and clientele are concentrated. In cities like London or Frankfurt such centres can be easily identified. They can also be found in Lyon, Düsseldorf and Munich, although as somewhat smaller versions. These international finance and services centres are globally interlinked and form part of the much quoted global city network.

Modern R & D spaces ('Technopoles'): These are urban quarters, or regional territories and spaces, where public and private R & D institutions are located, where they carry out basic and applied research, where a variety of institutions of higher education and permanent education provide the required skilled labour force for laboratories and training establishments. Centred around such spaces are high income housing areas, leisure clubs and sports facilities for the R & D work force The prototype model of such R&D spaces is the Silicon Valley around Stanford University. European examples of such specialized districts are Oxford and Cambridge in Britain, Sophia-Antipolis in the vicinity of Nice, Louvain-la-Neuve in Belgium, and Garching in Munich or the new technology complex in Dortmund.

Traditional industrial complexes: All over Europe traditional industrial areas are still in a process of gradual restructuring. Some are more successful in changing their obsolete or continuously subsidized economic base. Others have become the favourite location of power plants, waste disposal facilities and marginalized scrap and recycling industries. Some are still producing basic industrial products, which do not require a sophisticated labour force or easy access to airports or modern logistics centres. Others, finally, make use of the abundant derelict industrial space for storage and logistical operations which would be more costly elsewhere. The obvious examples of such spaces are coal and steel regions, such as parts of the Ruhr in Germany or La Loraine in France. Others are derelict port areas in London, Liverpool, Genua, Marseille or Rostock. Additionally, in most metropolitan regions such quarters can be found reminding us of what we tend to forget, namely that Paris and Berlin have always been industrial headquarters providing a considerable number of jobs for a skilled urban labour force.

Modern production complexes ('just-in-time regions'): In contrast with old industrial areas, modern industrial complexes are characterized by modern infrastructure, new production plants in a key sector (mainly automobile, but also defence, aerospace consumer electronics etc.) and a variety of smaller and medium-sized supplier plants. The complex is additionally complemented by all kinds of producer-orientated public and private services, from education and training to insurance and logistics. In Eisenach the new production centre of Opel/General Motors has caused the emergence of such a modern industrial complex. Others can be found not only in Wolfsburg (VW) and Regensburg (BMW), but also in Britain, France and Belgium.

Interregional distribution centres: Driven out by inner-city traffic limitations and favoured by just-in-time production technologies, interregional centres of logistics and wholesale distribution are emerging at suitable out-of-town locations, linked to interregional transportation corridors and near former inner-European boundaries. Such centres are strategic hubs for Europe-wide logistical operations, or out-of-town centres for consumer goods distribution within the city region. In their vicinity transport-related production and services tend to be located, such as gasoline stations, truck selling and maintenance operations, cheap accommodation, as well as wholesale distribution and teleshopping and home delivery enterprises.

Urbanized transportation corridors: Along trans-European motorways, easily accessible from a national or European point of view, developments take place that accelerate the gradual urbanization of the corridor. Their accessibility (by car) favours firms and households driven out by inner urban restructuring and exorbitant rents to locate at a motorway exit one community after the other. Enterprises benefiting from the flexible labour force living at such locations and from generous local government subsidies follow. As a consequence, the former rural landscape is gradually urbanized. The corridor along the Rhine valley in Germany is such an example; others can be found in the Rhone or Danube valleys in France and Austria, respectively.

Urban backwater spaces: All city regions in Europe have backwater spaces where urban functions are concentrated and although they are considered to potentially spoil the image of the city they are indispensable for the city to function. These are urban quarters where, for various reasons (industrial dereliction, social erosion etc.), land values and housing rents are low, where the land market does not raise speculative hopes, where an outdated urban infrastructure is in bad shape, and where environmental conditions are deplorable. Such urban areas are 'ideal' locations for low-cost urban operations and marginal businesses. But for many urban dwellers they are the only remaining affordable urban space. Hence they are the quarters of the urban underclass, of ethnic minorities and businesses, and for any urban functions which require inner urban locations at low costs.

Rural industrial complexes: Future agricultural production in Europe will be industrial in character, and where soil conditions and topography are favourable. Such areas will be dominated by large-scale privately owned farms and related agro-businesses with all the necessary forward and backward linkages and agricultural services.

Marginalized rural regions: As a result of mainstream European integration policies, rural regions with low agricultural production located in the geographical periphery of Europe and in the shadow of major trans-European transportation corridors or with limited accessibility to a major European city region will be further marginalized. Few economic prospects remain for such regions. They may become European nature reserves, if there is a certain ecological potential. They may have a chance of becoming second and third-home regions for the affluent European households, and they may sell their remoteness for all kind of activities which do not require centrality or which are not welcome at central locations (e.g. nuclear power plants, defence-related facilities, bio-genetic experimental laboratories or industrial waste disposal facilities).

Gentrified rural areas: Rural areas near city regions tend to become gentrified by urbanites who aim for a rural lifestyle at an easily accessible nearby location. The more attractive the rural landscape is and the more the local production is threatened by lower world market prices, the more likely is it that agricultural production is given up. Apart from a few remaining city farms selling untreated natural products at higher prices to nearby consumers, such regions tend to be taken over gradually by citizens who wish to live in a environmentally sound rural environment, at first only over the weekend and then maybe permanently after early retirement.

Aerovilles ('airport cities'): The easy accessibility to international airports has caused airport development corporations and private developers to invest in airport cities, where airport-related services and firms requiring fast access to global transport networks find suitable locations for their business activities. Apart from in Japan and North America such airport cities, which are simultaneously centres of global logistics, are developed or under development in Amsterdam, Paris and Frankfurt, in London or in Stockholm.

Leisure worlds ('Disney worlds'): Eurodisney, recently renamed 'Disneyland, Paris', is a prominent example of the kind of leisure complexes that seem to emerge all over Europe with more or less economic success. They may have the form of 'Centre Parks' which offer easily accessible and affordable short-term holidays in a relaxed but organized atmosphere no more than two hours away from home. They may be entertainment parks for a weekend visit with children, or areas of organized sport and recreation for short-term and longer-term holidays (e.g. yachting, golf, horse riding or skiing).

Such spatial categories are most likely to emerge in one or the other form in most European city regions (Figure 3.1). Knowing the economic pattern of a particular city region these categories can be easily mapped. These spatial categories are linked into interregional, international or even global information networks. They develop their own dynamics and infrastructural requirements, and they perfectly reflect the growing fragmentation of western society, where spatial competition clearly rules the game. As a rule the respective functional specialization is mutually reinforced once the particular image of such spaces is established.

There is much empirical evidence that the development trends sketched above favour spatial polarization trends. Polarization means that there are territorial units which benefit from certain trends and urban regional competition, and others which have to bear all or some negative implications of specialization and spatial differentiation. Such trends can be observed at all levels of decision-making, at the European and the national, at the regional and the urban levels. A few examples may illustrate such polarization processes.

The European level: For historical reasons the regional disparities within Europe are still considerable. However they are being measured, in terms of the Gross National Product (GNP), household income or long-term unemployment, in accessibility to education or in R&D employment, the disparities between the regions in Europe are still considerable. While the structurally weak regions of the European Union, both agricultural and traditionally industrial regions, have some chance to benefit from European regional policies, the regions of Eastern Europe have to rely on their own potential and efforts - cheap labour being the most effective these days. There is some evidence that the polarization trends within the enlarged European Union, while still growing for the time being, will ultimately stop or may even be reversed in the long run. The disparities between regions in Eastern Europe and those more affluent regions in Germany, Italy,

Switzerland or Denmark will still remain visible and measurable for a few more decades to come.

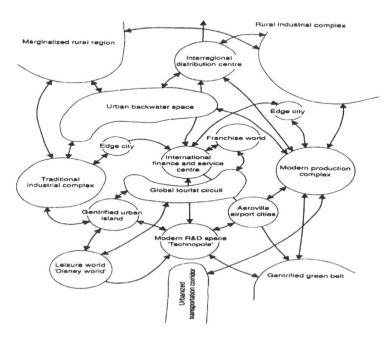

Figure 3.1 The spatial structure of the European city region in the 1990s

Source: Author's own draft

The national level: National governments, which have to ensure that their national spatial development responds to both European integration and regionalism, do not have an easy task. With the gradual decline of the nation-State they increasingly and necessarily delegate power to the European level, and to the regional or even local level. Now, affluent regions and cities use their own potential, power and initiatives to benefit from the globalizing economy and regional or urban competition, while weaker regions and cities, with only limited endogenous potential, have little chance to withstand the global competition. Their only remaining chance is to link into the wider European network of city regions. Otherwise these regions continue to be drained of their skilled and active labour force. At the close of the vicious circle of emigration and disinvestments, these regions become clearly marginalized and vulnerable for environmental corruption.

The regional level: Spatial differentiation processes sketched above will separate the region into urban glamour and backwater areas with their respective privileged and underprivileged urban classes. Land values in urban regions tend to explode in certain locations. While land values in some socially and aesthetically privileged quarters of a central city or of selected high-income suburbs grow to exclusive heights, they tend to stagnate in other parts of a region where environmental pollution or social erosion prevent middle-high-income households from investing and settling. The result is a growing social fragmentation of city regions, where single urban districts tend to become virtually or even physically walled into social and ethnic communities like isolated islands in an urban archipelago.

The urban level: The social fragmentation of cities is a phenomenon which was considered to be overcome by the modern European welfare state. Now it is reappearing in all European cities. There are growing income disparities of ever smaller urban households and an increasing number of individuals living below the poverty line. The growing number of the homeless is a visible sign of the decline of social housing all over Europe. Ethnic minorities and substandard quarters emerge which are distinct from those urban quarters shown in international city promotion brochures. Security issues are becoming the prime concern of city dwellers and investors. The mainstream deregulation spirit in Western Europe and the resulting denunciation of it accelerates such processes of social erosion in cities. Constrained by public sector deficits, the cities will not be able to compensate for national or regional policies, which deny the need for some form of public intervention, redistribution and social cushioning. Urban pockets of organized crime, power and urban poverty will appear side by side with office quarters and middle-class housing. Images of fragmented American cities have always been seen as non-transferable to Europe. Now first signs of similar developments can be observed in the suburbs of Paris, in Glasgow or in Milan. Most likely, they will also emerge in Berlin.

Which Developments Will Affect Spatial Change in Europe?

The present space-functional division of labour in Europe is the outcome of two millennia of territorial history, of wars and marriages, of feudal dominance, creativity and exploitation, of trading patterns and civic pride, of urban cultures and rural traditions. The spatial result of this long evolutionary process is a complex system of nations and regions, of urban hierarchies and transport and communication networks. As a rule the further development of this spatial system is mainly determined by economic forces and political intervention, while cultural traditions may just retard or accelerate ongoing capitalistic development processes. The means of intervening in this system are weak and time is crucial. Hence, most probably, Europe in the year 2046, i.e. in 50 years from now, will not look very different from today's Europe, assuming that the ethnic conflicts in Bosnia will not spread to Europe as a whole, that the project Europe will continue to appeal to citizens and decision-makers in Europe and that, *cum grano salis*, ongoing economic development trends will continue.

The change will be more obvious in the cities and regions of Eastern Europe, where the legacies of half a century of State-controlled economic development are quite visible in space. And such changes will undoubtedly be further accelerated where and when the politically desired and envisaged enlargement of the European Union to Eastern Europe takes place. Western Europe, in turn, will just experience a further extrapolation of existing spatial trends, as sketched above. The territorial changes here will be visible on the micro- rather than on the macro level.

There is much speculation and insufficient empirical research as yet on the driving forces as the key factors of spatial change at the European level. The European Commission legitimizes its European regional policy efforts, and the considerable budget linked to it, with the hope that its policy will in the end contribute to a further cohesion of social and economic space in Europe. Others have expressed their doubts about the efficiency of such intervention, asking for further deregulation and the acceptance of letting market forces determine where development takes place.

Apart from the extensively described spatial implications of globalization and new technologies, there are some additional Europe-wide development trends which will have long-term effects on the spatial functional division of tasks over the European territory as a whole. These trends will change the structure of cities and city regions, both in the centre and the periphery of the Continent. Where they will materialize, however, is difficult to say. It will very much depend upon local circumstances and policies. The most evident developments with a potential spatial influence are briefly discussed in the following section of this paper.

The Completion of the Trans-European High-speed Rail Network. At present considerable efforts are being undertaken to create a network of efficient transportation corridors across (mainly Western) Europe, allowing high-speed trains to cut on Continental travel times and goods being transported across Europe with fewer environmental impacts. This is done by upgrading existing infrastructure and by promoting the construction of missing links to complete already existing networks, such as the TGV network in France, or the ICE lines in Germany. An efficient trans-European transport network is rightly considered to be an essential precondition for an integrated European market.

Now most larger cities and regions in Europe are competing and lobbying to be comfortably linked to this new network. They are well aware that this link will be crucial for economic survival in the competitive European market in the 21st century . Being de-linked from this high-speed network would mean losing accessibility and, as a consequence, the loss of headquarters functions, a qualified expert labour force, inward investment, media coverage and international image - such losses will mean remaining in the shadow of regional economic development. The earlier cities are served by the system, the better their competitive advantages as attractive European locations for economic activities. However, this high-speed rail network will also contribute to a further spatial polarization in Europe, and even more so if the high-speed rail network is linked to international airports. This is already the case in Paris and Lyon, and a rail network will soon be opened in Frankfurt (in the year 2004). Consequently city regions in Europe will, as a rule, grow faster where the new trans-European infrastructure is available at an early date. Where global and European accessibility for face-to-face contacts is maximized, the further expansion of the city region can be anticipated. However, present political concerns in the Member States of the European Union (unemployment increases, Maastricht II etc.) and the financial crisis in the public sector all over Europe are not favourable environment for huge infrastructure investments, such as the trans-European network.

The Unlimited Growth of International Airport Complexes. Besides high-speed train stops, the quality of air transport accessibility is considered to be another key location factor and a priority issue in global city competition. Although, as a rule, hindered by local citizen groups, airport corporations all over Europe aim at improving the efficiency and global accessibility of their airports. Adding runways and terminals to allow for an unlimited 24-hour service and increasing the number of departures and landings is their dream, which in Europe, however, rarely comes true (with the exception of Paris and London). Being, or becoming, a hub in the global network is what they aim at. This would attract airlines and allow daily services to a wide range of European destinations. This, in turn, would bring about the quantity which is necessary for further expansionist strategies. Development trends show that the airports have become the nodes and key engines of economic development in city regions. Airport cities are evolving, and with them the spatial structure of city regions is slowly changing. What the railway station was in the 19th century for the medieval city, The airport complexes will be for the city region in the 21st century what the railway station was in the 19th century for the medieval city, i.e., a reorientating of functions in what becomes a much wider space.

As a rule, any new major investment in Europe, be it in high-quality office space or industrial production, in large-scale shopping centres or in entertainment industries, will be not further away than 100 to 200 km (one to max. two hours access time) from an efficient international airport (and its high-speed railway link). This in turn will put further development pressure on the already densely populated city regions in Europe. They will slowly change their monocentric structure into polyycentric conurbations, where attractive small and medium-size towns will gain at the expense of the central city, while underprivileged backwater spaces will absorb all the utilities and blue-collar workers. Such spaces are necessary to maintain the proper functioning of the city region and to provide the necessary local services for the city's global agenda.

The Spatial Implications of New Telecommunication Technologies. There is still much uncertainty around the most likely spatial consequences of new telecommunication technologies. Will their decentralization potential contribute to relieve core cities from further development pressure? Will it promote the reduction of personal mobility and thereby contribute to a more sustainable Europe? Will it bring about new chances for peripheral and underprivileged areas in Europe? Or will it rather strengthen the ongoing spatial centralization process, as the diffusion of the new technology originates from the globalized centres? There is some evidence for all these possibilities.

Indeed, there is much potential in the new technology to allow certain highly skilled households, liberal professions, artists and small specialized firms to locate themselves wherever they wish to be and to live, in Tuscany or Smaland, in the Massif Central or in Tyrol. It needs little imagination to anticipate a coincidence of attractive landscapes with a certain concentration of such 'footloose' jobs. Whether these groups will permanently decentralize or just do so on a part-time basis (in winter, or in summer, for three months or just five times a year) or only when they finally retire is not known. It may well be that the remote job facility, made possible by new telecommunication technologies, is just an additional option for a certain time period, not a serious alternative for a permanent job dislocation.

There is equal evidence that the new telecommunication technologies will strengthen the already economically viable city regions, where such technologies are first introduced (German examples are Frankfurt and Info-City Rhein-Ruhr). The dialectics of spatial freedom and independence, and the growing wish for more face-to-face contacts needs a large choice of opportunities for such contact, and can be found only in the international, multicultural ambience of a large city region where permanent cultural and entertainment events take place, where live world music and world food, world theatre and world sport can be enjoyed.

However, as the new technologies are just at the brink of being widely used and distributed, reliable empirical information on the real spatial implications of the massive use of these new technologies can only be measured in only ina decade or so. Much comparative research has still to be done to transform informed guesswork into empirical evidence

The Removal of Inner-European Borders. There will be spatial changes in inner-European border regions, where the removal of administrative and physical barriers will potentially create new investment conditions for selected industries (logistics, warehousing, food industries). Regions which due to their former national remoteness have been neglected in the past will gain from their new European centrality.

Investors will benefit from easy access to two (or even three) markets, from the bilinguality of job seekers, and from the financial support such regions receive. For households, too, it will be not only easier but also cheaper to find and obtain permanent (or weekend) housing on whatever side they please. Cooperation between border communities will be facilitated and intensified. It will result in joint operation of utilities or public services in border regions.

Such trends and activities will slightly increase development pressure in border regions. Cities in such regions (Strasbourg, Aachen, Arnheim, Karlsruhe, Bolzano, Dover, Calais) will experience increased interest.

Immigration and Integration? Many right-wing political parties in Europe use the fear of a growing number of immigrants to promote their populist policies. Affluent Europe is the target of considerable migration flows from Arab- and black Africa, from the Middle East and from all over Eastern Europe and Central Asia. Both push and pull factors cause this migration. Although the conditions immigrants experience in Europe, onçe they have arrived in the quarters where they can settle down, are usually below their original expectations, the migration will continue as long as the living (and political) conditions in their home countries are still below any low-class standards in Europe, and despite all concerted efforts to make the exterior boundaries of Europe less penetrable.

The numbers of immigrants are considerable. In 1994, more than 200,000 ethnic Germans came to Germany from the former territory of the Soviet Union and Eastern Europe. In 1990, 4 million migrants lived in France, originating mainly from the North African Magreb States and the former French colonies in Africa. All over Europe large cities (Paris, Berlin, Vienna, Frankfurt) and gateway cities (Salonikki, Marseille) suffer most from such immigration flows. The implications for these cities and regions are considerable. Housing and jobs have to be provided, as well as education and health services. They all draw on public funds and give rise to emotional competition at the lower income end of the society. In France the resulting tensions have recently forced the government to launch a comprehensive support programme for the French suburbs, where the concentration of foreign immigration has reached a level which local communities could not cope with any more.

Urban and Regional Competition. The ongoing urban and regional competition in Europe fostered by planning consultants and marketing agencies has lead to an abundance of image and public relation campaigns which aim to sell a city or a region to ill-specified outside target groups. They aim at selling the potentials of the city and region to potential inward investors and international property developers. Some cites (Glasgow, Rotterdam, Lille, Toulouse or Karlsruhe) are more active in this respect than others. The focus on competition in turn sets new urban priorities and requires public investments. As a consequence flagship projects (convention centres, shopping precincts, museums etc.) and media coverage of international events (garden festivals, international conventions, Olympic games, festivals, cultural city of Europe, etc.) receive more political attention and support, and a larger share of public funds, than less spectacular projects of the local social agenda. This also leads to a better linking of such cities to European transport and communication networks. To market the success, success stories are written and disseminated. A new image evolves and local citizens identify with the new image and develop renewed civic pride. Property developers are one of the key actors in such games. The competition as such does not cause major spatial changes. However, spatial changes inevitably happen in the inner cities and regenerated port areas, causing upper-class income households to return to the revitalized inner city ('gentrification') and driving low income households out of town to unattractive suburban residents' quarters. The result is considerable spatial shifts within the city region. In the end, despite all negative effects, it cannot be denied that such activities place those best-selling cities better on the mental map of European actors searching for geographic targets of new capital investment.

A Paradigm Shift of European Agricultural Policies? Present Western European agriculture is (similar to that of Japan or the USA) very much based on price- and quantity-related agricultural policies, eating up 75% of the European Union's budget. As a rule, this policy has favoured the large (industrialized) farmer at the cost of the environment and the small farm. There is growing dissatisfaction with such a policy and first efforts are being made to reward more sustainable farming and to promote quality instead of quantity. The ultimate goal of the proponents of such cautious experiments is to shift the focus from agricultural production to landscape conservation. They receive unexpected support when the further extension of the European Union to Eastern Europe is being discussed. The application of the present agricultural policy to Eastern Europe with its huge mechanized agricultural complexes would immediately cause the Commission´s budget to go bankrupt and ruin the majority of less competitive Western European farmers. A total paradigm change in agricultural policy, however, would change the rationality of agricultural land use all over Western Europe. To what extent such changes would open up agricultural land for development has not yet been researched. It may be worthwhile to explore the potential changes in order to anticipate the consequences such changes may have for cities and regions in Western Europe.

The Emergence of a New Regionalism? All over Europe (from Scotland to Normandy, from Bavaria to Catalonia) there is much evidence of a growing regionalism, where identifiable local traditions, local languages and local cultures are regaining renewed respect. Justified as local protection against anonymous internationalism, the new regionalism does receive more and more political support from the whole political spectrum from right to left. The new appeal to regionalism is also reflected in the recent establishment of a European Committee of Regions parallel to the European Parliament.

The new self-confidence of regions is strongly rooted in those segments of the regional population which have close ties with the landscape and regional culture.

What will be the long-term spatial effects of this new regionalism? Although any agreement on what defines a modern region at the turn of the millennium is hard to reach, the move may offer new chances for intra-regional development, for securing the permanence of regional firms, for the development of endogenous local resources, for cultural activities which draw on local and regional traditions and contrast them with international movements. The new regionalism strengthens regional identities and images, which in turn support regional marketing for both tourism and inward investment. The more the regional population identifies with their regional life spaces, the more they will seek to live and to work in the region. This in turn will facilitate the conservation of the regional landscape and its historical heritage.

There may be additional trends causing visible spatial implications over limited time periods in combination with the trends sketched above: new leisure-oriented lifestyles emerging from the Hollywood dream factories and Disney laboratories may put new pressure on the urban fringe to provide a wider choice of organized outdoor recreation facilities. Energy conservation policies, together with new organizational forms of transport (car sharing etc.) could contribute to new travel patterns and result in changing locational choices of households. Such changes may also be the consequence of new forms of work organization. New logistical concepts will change the logics of goods distribution in city regions. In the end it will be a question of the extent to which such trends are occurring, whether their spatial implications are visible and measurable, and whether their effects can only be observed at certain locations and regions, or be considered in terms of Europe-wide implications.

Scenarios for Future Spatial Development in Europe

How will Europe develop in the first half-century of the next millennium? There is no single answer to this question. At present one can read much about what the implications of the acceptance of new members to the European Commission will be for Europe as a whole. The debate centres mainly on a two- (or more) speed Europe, where early members and winners of the European Single Market Project form their own club and go ahead, following their liberal market paradigms, while the losers, or those who have not even been granted access to the European Union, form their own respective strategic alliances to join the club at the earliest convenience.

Two issues will remain for some more time on the European agenda: secure jobs and a sustainable environment. Obviously, there are no easy or sectoral recipes defining how these two goals can be achieved, although there is much actionism on the political agenda. There are indeed no easy ways to reach such goals and the long way ahead is full of obstacles, impediments and stumbling blocks that need to be removed.

It is certain that the further deregulation of European regulatory systems, the cutting down of welfare systems, the creation of new élites and the deliberate revival of the two-class society will not make European Industries and services more competitive in Asia. Such policies, favoured by mainstream economists and policy-makers, will soon turn out to produce cul-de-sac situations, although they have undoubtedly contributed to making the public sector more flexible, more creative and more effective. Given the speed of economic and human development in Asia it is unlikely that Europe, with a different history, with different value systems and lifestyles among its population, will ever have a chance to be competitive in this race for cheaper production costs and cheaper products. The ultimate result of such policies would be social polarization similar to that in the competing countries and unacceptable in an environment where human rights are well established. In the end, given the cultural differences between Europe and Asia, Europe would be rather the loser of this race. Drastic policies to redistribute jobs among the European society, with the help of new regulatory measures (reduced and flexible working hours, flexible wage systems, alternative pension systems etc.), may in the end be the only solution. There is little hope that global free-trade paradigms will be given up and be replaced by more protective trade policies, in which ban the import of Asian goods to Europe; a move which is hardly conceivable under present circumstances. The banana quota policy of the European Union illustrates the difficulties of such regulatory policies. Hence the Continent has to be more creative in the use of its own endogenous potentials (history, culture, human capital, research etc.)

As already stated earlier, the space-functional division of tasks will not dramatically change in Europe, no matter to what political direction the Continent moves. As a rule, spatial changes will happen in a few regions only, in city regions, in some border areas, and in regions where attractive natural features will attract mobile households and liberal professions. Over longer periods the spatial changes will be faster in Eastern than in Western Europe. In this respect Europe will move more and more towards American and Japanese conditions, where turnover times in urban development are much shorter than in Europe, and with the consequence that land use and the physical appearance of cities change within decades rather than centuries.

The following five spatial scenarios for Europe are deliberately provocative. Some just extrapolate and exaggerate known spatial development trends, others are rather normative scenarios, which open up windows for the formulation of new spatial development paradigms in Europe.

Euro-megalopolis. Prevailing development trends suggest that the globalization of the economy will cause a further concentration of urban power and activities in Europe. The consequence could be that Europe in the 21st century is dominated by a huge, fully urbanized Euro-megalopolis (Figure 3.2) consisting of a few cooperating global command centres (Paris, London, Brussels, Frankfurt) together with their adjacent urban regions (Randstad, Rhein-Ruhr, Berlin, Padonia). Efficient intra-metropolitan transport and telecommunication systems would link the activity nodes of the polycentric Euro-megalopolis to allow easy accessibility from international airports and comfortable movements within its territory. Nature conservation, outdoor recreation, provision of water and production for local consumption would be tasks left to the European cities and regions outside the Euro-megalopolis. To a certain extent such a Euro-megalopolis reflects the spatial expression of a two-speed Europe. It is in the political, economic, financial command centres of the megalopolis where European information and media power is concentrated, where economic development is promoted to meet the challenge of competing Asian metropolitan regions (Tokyo, Kansai, South China, Greater Bangkok, Singapore or Java).

The remaining European spaces outside the Euro-megalopolis remain as the reproduction spaces of the 50 million people living in the mega-region.

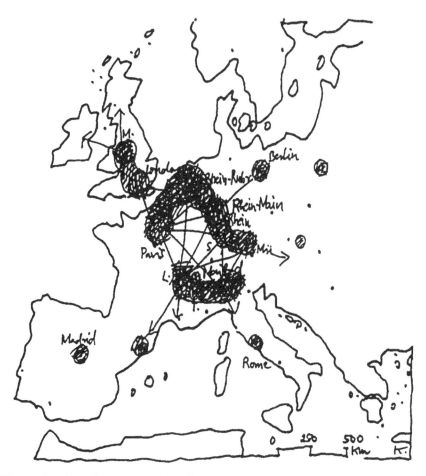

Figure 3.2 The Euro-megalopolis

Source: Author's own draft

Theme Park Europe? There are good arguments for perceiving Europe in the 21st century to be the prime tourist target for Asian tourists, searching for unspoiled mediaeval townscapes, romantic city tours and feudal city-scapes. Europe as a huge theme park (Figure 3.3)? What speaks really against it? Why not? The unprecedented economic growth in Eastern and Southeastern Asia, followed by immense land speculation and out-of-scale urban developments, has whipped up local and regional cultures in their home regions - first in Japan, and now in Korea, Thailand, Malaysia and China. Now, the growing middle classes in that mega-region can afford to travel to Europe to the cradle of modernization, where they can see, what has irreversibly been destroyed in their home countries. Consequently city tourism, with all its economic forward-and-backward linkages, may become the main source of income for more and more European cities, both in Western as in Eastern Europe. Already today city tourism accounts for a considerable segment of jobs in cities such as Paris and London, Rothenburg and Heidelberg, Florence and Venice. Hence it may be wise to seriously consider this touristic option and to exploit the romantic search for visible and accessible history to secure jobs in a wide range of tourism-related branches. The growing touristic interest in European history will convince city fathers all over Europe of the need to reconsider their modernization policies. The assignment of European urban conservation zones, where all new development is carefully scanned as to their implications for tourism, may be one consequence of such a scenario. Obviously, some areas in Europe will benefit more than others from the Asian demand for vivid European history. Whether the Disney corporation will be asked to organize this European theme park remains a question of European pride.

Figure 3.3 Theme Park Europe

Source: Author's own draft

A Europe of Sustainable Regions? There is an obvious mismatch between the mobility goal of European economic integration and the popular sustainability vision. Many in-depth studies have proved, however, that sustainable development can only be achieved if unnecessary mobility is cut back. There is some hope now that new telecommunication technologies will contribute to the reduction of unnecessary mobility. Other strands of action are technological innovations to improve energy efficiency in transport and housing. Why not go even a step further? One could imagine a regulatory policy, in which mobility is reduced by the promotion of intraregional economic circuits. Such a policy for a region (in the size, say, of an average German *Bundesland* with a population of 5 to 8 million), could aim at producing 80% or more of all consumer products (food, household goods, furniture, office material etc.) within the region *(Buy regional!)*. Such a (high-tech subsistence) policy, made possible by new technologies which allow the production of simple goods almost anywhere in the world, would secure jobs in the region and it would cut unnecessary interregional transportation flows. The outcome of such a longer term policy would be a Europe of sustainable regions (Figure 3.4); of regions which, based on their endogenous potentials, would try to be as independent from importing consumer products from other regions as possible. On the other hand, these regions would have to specialize in products and services for which there is a global market, and for which the region has particular comparative advantages.

Figure 3.4 Europe of sustainable regions

Source: Author's own draft

Europe, Going East? Most known European spatial policy activities centre on Western Europe only. Eastern Europe is considered to be a territory where spatial development trends are still difficult to forecast, because the political systems are, in some cases, not yet fully stabilized and will remain so as long as local, regional and national economic development activities are still dominated by structural transformation processes. With or without the enlargement of the European Union to incorporate at least the Visegrad states (Poland, Czech Republic, Slovakia and Hungary) the development in a corridor of Central and Eastern European city regions reaching from Warsaw over Wroclaw (Breslau) to Prague and Budapest will be the favourite development corridor in Eastern Europe, whereby Berlin, Dresden, Nuremberg and Vienna may function as the exchange nodes between Eastern and Western Europe (Figure 3.5). The longer the considerable wage differential between Western and Eastern Europe exists, the faster will be the development process in Eastern Europe. Local industries will benefit from the outsourcing of Western European firms, tourism will benefit from very competitive prices, and construction industries from the demand for modernized housing, public facilities and production spaces. Thereby urbanized border regions adjacent to Western Europe will, in particular, be the target of new investments made possible by the exchange of cheaper goods and labour force and favoured by less rigid environmental regulations.

Figure 3.5 Europe, going East

Source: Author's own draft

Virtual Europe? Assuming that the decentralization potential of new technologies is fully utilized and that the new technology will be widely accepted and used practically by the next two generations of European households, liberal professions and small and medium-sized firms to organize life and work, Europe's spatial organization may look different from the way it looks now (Figure 3.1). Two spatial trends could be imagined. First, the larger European cities may become surrounded by information belts, which add a new ring of mixed activities to the city region beyond the existing green belts. Second, the traditional holiday regions of Europe along the Mediterranean and Baltic Seas, the Atlantic or in the Alps may slowly be transformed into permanent or semi-permanent multi-cultural residential communities, where new generations of flexible workers reside and work. The physical appearance of these urbanized belts and corridors will be a mélange of gentrified rural settlements, new suburban communities, edge cities and spaces for active recreation (golf, horse riding, yachting etc.), as one can already find in California today. Their European accessibility from international airports or high-speed rail stops is essential; the local provision of efficient and reliable public services is of course guaranteed.

Figure 3.6 Virtual Europe

Source: Author's own draft

European Spatial Development: The Consequences for European Spatial Development Policies

What conclusions can be drawn from these scenarios for the further development of European spatial development policies? There is no doubt that the cohesion goal remains valid and a first priority of European integration. However, as redistribution policies have lost some of their appeal to the European society, additional supporting ideas have to be developed and disseminated. Since the fall of the Berlin wall the Project Europe has lost its momentum. Whether there will be a new generation of visionary policy makers and opinion leaders coming into power at the European level is uncertain in the present political climate. Routine management seems to have political priority in order to calm down those citizens in Western Europe afraid of losing what they have inherited (employment, the Deutschmark, the language, the culture, or individual mobility). Hence, the speed of implementing the European Project has been reduced. This reduced speed, however, opens up new chances to think more about the role spatial policies could have in shaping a sustainable European territory.

The only realistic chance European spatial development policies have, if they realistically wish to influence spatial development processes at the macro scale, is the production of spatial images of a sustainable Europe. Such images, supported by regional policy measures, demonstrate the validity of the spatial images and by critical spatial monitoring could guide the day-to-day policies at all decision-making levels in Europe.

The suggestions made for possible European scenarios have led to a few visions of potential future spatial images in Europe. With some probability the European space in the 21st century will be characterized by a combination and overlapping of these spatial scenarios.

Spatial planning and spatial policies at a macro level have only a modest chance to influence the locational logics of the market economy. They can create and enforce off-limit zones for uncontrolled development, although only if they also can organize means to cushion the negative social impacts of non-investments. They can promote and finance infrastructure developments to provide the infrastructural conditions for private investment. They can produce spatial images as mental guidelines for political decision-making processes. And, finally, they can use their spatial information power, resulting from intensive spatial monitoring, as early spatial warning systems, to inform the public about spatial developments which conflict with their value systems and their accepted development guidelines. Existing institutional arrangements which allow such tasks to be fulfilled need to be assessed, and comparative research to increase the knowledge about spatial development in a global economy has to be promoted. Otherwise, the credibility of spatial planning will continue to remain weak.

Note

1   Revised version of the paper given at the workshop. First published in: International Planning Studies, Vol. 1, No.2, 1996, 143 -163; Carfax Publishing Limited, PO Box 25, Abingdon Oxfordshire OX14 3UE, UK.

References

Ache, P., Bremm, H.-J. & Kunzmann, K.R. (1991) Auswirkungen des Europäischen Binnenmarktes auf die Raum- und Siedlungsstruktur in Westdeutschland, Schriftenreihe Forschung des Bundesministeriums für Raumordnung, Bauwesen und Städtebau, No.448, Bonn.

ARL/DATAR (1992) Perspektiven einer Europäischen Raumordnung (Perspectives of Regional Development Policy in Europe). Hannover: Verlag der Akademie für Raumforschung und Landesplanung).

BFLR (Bundesforschungsanstalt für Landeskunde und Raumordnung) (1995) Trendszenarien der Raumentwicklung in Deutschland und Europa. Bonn: BFLR.

Brunet, Robert (1989) Les Villes Européenes. Paris: La Documentation Francaise.

COM (Commission of the European Communities) (1991) Europe 2000: Outlook or the Development of the Community's Territory. Luxemburg: Office for the Publication of the European Communities.

COM (Commission of the European Communities) (1992) Europe 2000k+: European Cooperation for Territorial Development. Luxemburg: Office for the Publication of the European Communities.

CoE (Council of Europe) (1983) A Regional/Spatial Charter for Europe. Strasbourg:CoE.

Kunzmann, Klaus R., (1993a) Geodesign: Chance oder Gefahr? in: Informationen zur Raumentwicklung, Heft 7: Planungskartographie und Geodesign, pp.389-396.

Kunzmann, Klaus R., (1993b) Konsequenzen der Europäischen Integration für die Entwicklung von Städten und Regionen in der Bundesrepublik Deutschland. In: Raumentwicklung. Politik für den Standort Deutschland. Materialien zur Raumentwicklung, Heft 57, pp.79-86.

Discussion by: Heinz Fassmann

Klaus Kunzmann's paper is an introductory one which does not include any of the following: figures, detailed research results, quantitative projections, calculated scenarios or any precise descriptions of spatial and societal processes. The paper analyses the main factors of structuring the European urban system and offers ideas for future development.

The starting point of the discussion on future development is the observation that our economic system has reached a new stage. Compared with the last eighty to fifty years, the engine of our economic development is no longer the mass production of industrial products. Nowadays, more and more profit can be made by utilizing the information processed by financial services, by taking advantage of global locations as well as the global diversification of manufactured goods. Regions become specialized and cities gain more and more privileged positions in a global economic system.

The privileged position of the urban centre is based on information and transportation flows. Cities are the nodes of different information and transportation networks. Information is collected and processed in the cities. Firms and enterprises located in the metropoles have better access to information and transportation networks, and therefore they are able to make more profit. Compared with other locations, the cities have clear comparative advantages.

Kunzmann emphazises these trends towards increasing spatial specialization resulting in spatial differentation and - because of very uneven profit rates - growing polarization. Polarization can be observed on three different levels: on the national, regional and urban levels. Kunzmann describes these different levels and he argues that they are highly interlinked.

The global economy with its global specialization leads unavoidably to a further growth of the urban regions in Europe, and to growing polarization between them and the rural and peripherial regions. The paper could be more analytical and precise in defining the keyfactors for the different development of the urban regions. The question is, which urban region will grow faster than another? Can Vienna increase its functional position within a European urban system, or will Prague, Budapest, Munich or Milan develop more successfully? Kunzmann offers some factors which will affect spatial change in general (not only the urban regions) in Europe: the European high-speed rail network, the growth of international airports, the development of new information technologies or the success of selling the potentials and images of cities and regions. One can add to these the attractiveness for the leisure society, the qualifications of the labour force or the existence of a critical mass of future-orientated firms.

It is interesting to analyse the importance of the different factors. On this point the paper offers more or less eclectical footnotes. Some are very important and convincing, others are not. Why immigration and integration, for example, are said to be the main factors for regional change is not understandable. They are important but, compared to other factors, there is some doubt whether they are the main factors.

The paper ends with some scenarios visualizing very different future developments. Kunzmann shows extreme scenarios which probably will never become true, but they do offer interesting starting points for thinking about and discussing future development. The primary value of Kunzmann's paper is to be found in exactly this objective.

PART II:
POLICIES

4 Policies without Inexpert Regulation and Partial Anarchy

BENNY HJERN

Introduction

Should a general thesis of the article be Stated in minimal fashion, it would read: Basic professional influence in spatial transformation processes in Europe is already (with variegated skills) placed with local (private and public) actors. In abbreviated form the theoretical underpinning of the thesis is, firstly, that economic growth develops in local processes (but not necessarily by local actors alone) and, secondly, that, to the extent central governments or EU are able to help economic growth along, it is by strengthening local processes (not necessarily with funds) so that entrepreneurs may keep control of their original definition of ideas. If, in the end, regionalization were to provide positive inputs into economic growth processes, it is unlikely to be founded on existing European 'regions'. Most of them are constructs, mainly for administrative control purposes of States, with little significance for creative economic or democratic developments. Positive inputs are more likely to stem from regionalization from below, in spatial areas of functional economics and not fromadminstrative units of States.

Innovative developments in economics and politics are usually local, depending on local definitions of the situation and local entrepreneurs (but not necessarily on local ideas and resources only). Important existing patterns of economic activity and political culture were established locally, well before the advent of European welfare States. The constitutions of modern States are founded on local government.

Currently, it is only the constitution of the Bavarian Republic that formally acknowledges this foundation of democratic States, but the constitutions of European States do at least infer a municipal foundation of democratic politics. Here is an example:

In the first Municipal Act of Austria (1849) it is Stated that: 'the fundament of the free State is the free municipality'.

The clause is also included in Austria's present Municipal Act (Gemeindeverfassungsgesetz 1962). In the recent constitutional discussions (Stärkung des Föderalismus) started before Austria applied for EU membership, some argued that it is now finally about time to review principles that have made Austrian federalism stop before the municipalities (cf. Häussl 1994, 'Föderalismus darf nicht vor Gemeinden halt machen'). Other countries have had similiar discussions on the constitutional position of local government within post-Maastricht democracy. However, established forces of centralization in European welfare States are used to treat municipalities not as free but as local administrative units of the State (federal or unitary).

For a long time politicians, as well as scholars in economics and politics, have looked upon the national economy and the nation State as the focus of action and as the unit of analysis in investigations to such an extent that the micro-foundations of economics and democratic politics enter policy-making as assumptions only or, when empirically assessed, to compose aggregate models to handle national economies or predict national elections better. There is, however, much to suggest that 'micro-foundations', such as firms and local governments are, if not as easily as before, transformable into national averages of economics and politics. Studies demonstrate that 'coordination from below' and creative uses of State regulations by locals often correlate well with innovative economic and political developments. Studies also that the economic and political power of States is likely to be asymmetrical; that they are better able to confine than to create local democracy and economic development.

Meanwhile 'regions' are common units of analysis in economics. Much has been learnt about the economics of regions since the Laender, counties and other subnational units of States have become the focus of spatial development policy. By the middle of the 1980s, with the slogan, 'Europe of the Regions', this focus was forcefully transported onto the European level of (presumably) collaborating Member States. The transportation has effectively demonstrated the fuzziness of the concept across Europe. A fuzziness that may contribute to the political usefulness of 'region', but creates confusion in the analysis of spatial development. 'Region' seems to mean everything and therefore nothing (Cf. Hjern 1995, Harding 1996, Hogwood 1996 and Kneymeyer 1994).

'Region' has become a bastion of defence for some practitioners and theorists using the basic conservative optic, which was successfully applied in the Industrial Age to organize large manufacturing firms and welfare States, that 'orderliness hinges upon centrality' and, without which, they 'spot 'crises' wherever they look' (Luhmann 1982, p.xv).

Much in the recent European pre-occupation with regionalization suggests that 'region' is approached as an ersatz for 'State' by political élites and scholars, who finally have had to recognize that the assurance of centrality that the territorial State once provided is lost.

Europe would have been spared much post-Maastricht confusion had the catchword in the 1980s been 'Europe of the municipalities' rather than 'of the regions'. Politically European 'regions' are, at the moment, of many bewildering kinds. (German) States masquerading as 'regions', administrative planning districts of the State (with or without democratic facades attached to them), national 'regions' (more or less actively using strategies to decouple and federalize their States) or special regions of regulated State services of 'regions', are but a few examples. Few of these 'regions' fulfil the criteria of 'subnational units' as defined in the Treaty of Maastricht; but they are represented in the 'Committee of Regions' of the EU, as are municipalities, and they do live up to standards of democratic legitimacy and broad administrative jurisdiction set by the Treaty.

Paradoxically then, the Treaty of Maastricht, despite other shortcomings of clarity, defines the basic criteria for 'sub-national units' that lead back to the democratic roots of European States, i.e., the 'free municipality' as the fundament of democratic governance. But, as the present composition of the 'Committee of Regions' of EU demonstrates, the Treaty on this point is not taken seriously by Member States. How could it? In most European States the idea of democracy as based on 'free municipalities' has been reduced to panegyric, selfserving exclamations by political and administrative managers of welfare States in decay.

As the legitimacy of centralized State authorities wanes in Western Europe, local political authorities, such as 'free municipalities', should take on a higher political significance. It is in local government that European democracy will have to start renewing itself soon - or not at all. All entrepreneurship is local, political and economic. Over the past decade, European political parties, established early in this century, have not succeeded in creating jobs and have demonstrated their inability to advance entrepreneurship of all kinds by applying the methods of the industrial society of the past. This means that, for at least a decade, local governments in Western Europe have had to carry the financial burdens of over-extended welfare States lacking in innovative ideas. If trends in proverbially centralistic, social democratic Sweden are representative, the solidarity of municipal departments with the national headquarters of established parties is rapidly dwindling. In past decades, Swedish municipalities have had to engage themselves, in an increasingly professional way, in a new and rapidly forming policy field, i.e., local industrial policy. This is partly because they have recognized the limitations of the State as an arbiter of economic and political developments, and partly because they are pushed to do so by global, if not necessarily European, economic trends.

Subsequent sections will point to some reasons why municipalities have had to engage themselves more vigorously in economic development strategies. It will be a narrative of how State regional policy has increasingly become but a factor in an emergent 'new' policy field in Europe: Local Industrial Policy (LIP).[1] The advent of LIP also re-introduces the broader issue of the functional division of labour between central and local government in a policy field, which is supposedly of such overarching macro-economic significance that, in Europe, the prerogative of the State to set priorities has remained unchallenged over a long period of time. At least in theory, because meanwhile it has been demonstrated, that even in the most 'Keynesian' of times, the practical role of the State was much humbler than depicted.

And if individual central governments have been less than effective in promoting LIP, why should they be more so as members of the European Union, i.e., the assembly of 20th century European l'ancien régimes?

L'ancien régimes: EU and redistributive regional policy

This article concerns phenomena, States, regions and development (economic and political) which, in the past ten years have come increasingly under review by scholars and political actors in Europe. It would seem that the evolving 'European Union' necessitated such re-examinations; but that is probably only partially true. Maastricht made it finally necessary to reflect upon evolutions long in the making, such as the inefficiency of centralizing State models and the loss of national economies or, for the sake of brevity and the purposes of this article, the problems with the territorial State as the unit of analysis in economics and as arbiter of political and economic spatial development.

For some time 'region' has evolved as a preferred unit of analysis of and action for 'spatial development policy'. However, regional policy analysis has focused on economic development only. Within the bounds of State models of the economy, there has been no strongly felt need to think of subnational political democracy as a necessary correlate to theories of regional economic development. Political 'regimes' are a constant in econometric models, and welfare State managers see 'regions' and municipalities as mandated to perform within State (or EU) programmes, and not as democratic units legitimized to organize strategies of economic development in their own right. Presumably then, regional development could be achieved by State programmes without the help of local government. Its involvement in economic development could, according to Swedish State managers, even reduce the effectiveness of national schemes (that were never properly evaluated for effectiveness in the first place). Meanwhile Sweden, in particular, and Europe as a whole, both suffer from deficits both in job-creation and democratic regeneration.

In its traditional form, regional policy was necessary for the political legitimacy of recent welfare States. Less dynamic regions (peripheries), suffering from global developments that affected spatial patterns of economic productivity were targeted for aid through political decisions well covered by the mass media. The political aim was to demonstrate to local 'victims' (of capitalism) that national decision-makers cared. (In Sweden, those sessions in Parliament in which regional policy was debated each year soon became known as 'folklore meetings'). Backbench members of Parliament made their speeches in one of those years to list the claims of the local district they would like to have in the records. Empirical indications that theories of redistributive regional policy were, at best, partial and beside the point politically (cf. articles in Andersson & Malmberg 1988 for a review of Nordic and European research).

Redistributive regional policy, expediently directed at political/administrative districts rather than economic 'regions', is a brainchild of the political élite of European States at the peak of the industrial era; that is, the period when large firms were considered to be national assets, allowing States to judge themselves affluent and to be the arbiters of economic developments. Now European States are struggling to overcome their economic reliance upon large, increasingly international firms, historically once pillars of their national economies and now the heralds of globalization and unemployment, if not outright industrial decline. The job-creation struggle of European welfare States is hampered by the fact that political institutions are leftovers from the age of industrialization. Particularly aggravating for the body politic of democratic States is the decline of party systems. Their rationalizations of political power and myths of authority provide no fundamental principles for social and economic organization any more.

Throughout this century, democratic States have been established in Western Europe. Members of these regimes now assemble in Brussels and Strasbourg. They represent the l'ancien régime of 20th century Europe. Like its 18th century counterpart, assembling in Vienna 1814-15, its fundamental principles of societal organization are out of date, possibly with the exception of initiatives for economic deregulation. The first European l'ancien régime was able, for some time, to defend privileges and stall ideas of economic and political reorganizations of society 'from below', until the break-through of democratic and industrial economic principles of organization from which present regimes have ensued. Will representatives of 20th century l'ancien régimes be able to uphold their centralistic notions of democracy and economic development with the help of the EU? Are there challenges 'from below' (and from analysts) with strategies that may help break through Europe's vicious circles of low job-creation capacity and 'illegitimate democracy' (for concept, cf. Hjern 1992)?

Is the EU as a 20th century l'ancien régime a functional equivalent of its 18th century counterpart at the Vienna Congress? With regard to regional policy, we suggest it is; at least judged by the Swedish case within the EU. So far, policy-makers, elevated from their capital cities to the heights of EU, have not become remarkably more creative in regional policy matters. Regional policy clings to centralistic, redistributive notions of past decades. The principles of European 'spatial development policy' closely resemble notions that, in the past, failed to institutionalize economic development in 'regions' of the Members States, but compared to Swedish regional policy, EU schemes are more programmatic).

In Sweden, EU policy is now smoothly adapted to benefit the same 'areas of development' that have been districts of regional policy for the past thirty years. Why should similiar notions create jobs as 'European policy' when they have failed to do so under Swedish colours? Just as national regional policy once should have helped 'peripheries' to identify with the politicial centre, so should European policy - presumably because of the way the EU supports national funds. In practice, however, local Swedish fund raising is part of a different strategy, namely, getting as much as possible of our national contributions back from Brussels. Regional policy, as an attempt to legitimize the EU, is a valid exercise in traditional redistributive politics, but it should not be confused with spatial development policy, whether national or European. Will the European Parliament soon stage its own 'folklore days' of regional policy?

Meanwhile it is doubtful if the legitimacy of either the EU, the Swedish or any other European l'ancien régime may be maintained or kept from dwindling further by means of regional policies, even if funds were available for the purpose to the extent they were over the past thirty years. Arguably they are not. With a preference for redistributive policies, including regional policy, EU and Member States may find themselves using increasingly more of their dwindling total resources on redistribution, thereby losing more and more of their ability to invest in expansive economic sectors, could these be easily defined (cf. Johansson 1993 and Nilsson 1995).

Inexpert State regulation and partial anarchy

The competence of the State's regulation of industrial and regional economic challenges is increasingly being called into questioned through theoretical and empirical arguments. The first mainly concern the volume of State intervention; the second, the effectiveness of measures. From within neo-classic economic theory, State activity with any kind of selective measures is hard to motivate. Other macro-economic theories are in need of supplementary political arguments. These have been hard to buttress with research because, among other things, studies have hardly been able to demonstrate the effectiveness and economic efficiency of selective economic policy. Regardless of its theoretical foundations, the political case for State regional policy is historically well established in European States. As argued above, regional policy developed within the redistributive political agenda of the welfare State. The idea to provide it with a buttress in economic theory has failed; and it is hard to rationalize even within political theory proper.

In Europe, the transformation from the liberal to the interventionist welfare State takes place in the period between 1930 and 1980. Wars notwithstanding, the period is characterized by unparallelled social and economic achievements due, among other things, to political and administrative institutions that greatly enhanced the State capacity for centralized mobilization, regulation and control of resources (a succinct analysis in Wittrock 1988). This centralizing State model functioned, and forged institutions for regulating social security programmes, as long as the role of selective measures was held back. The centralizing State model becomes exaggerated and counterproductive if applied to problems of a more selective kind for which the local environment more directly sanctions rational courses of action. Problems of regional policy belong to the selective mould. Applying the centralizing State model to regional policy problems therefore provides less systematic and measureable impacts than its adherents, mainly planners and traditional social democrats, claim on ist behalf.

Policy-makers and analysts usually establish themselves with the successful model of the era. The centralizing State model gives irregular results for industrial and regional policy problems, but as a macroeconomist (Leijonhuvfud 1981:307) argues, often analysts do not so much lead the world with their models as follow behind practice, trying to incorporate 'things that have been well-known for a long time ... into a logically consistent structure.' So although, in practice, the formation of local industrial policy increasingly coordinate and integrate State and EU programmes, a model of the decentralizing State and democratically accountable local government has been slow to develop in spatial development policy.

The consequences of an inappropriate use of the centralizing State model were discussed by the French sociologist, Durkheim, some hundred years ago (1893). He explicitly uses intervention in industrial activity as an example. The constitutional State, which is older than the interventionist State, based its arbitration on statutes. However refined and detailed, Durkheim (1964) observed that these would never catch up with the pace at which industrial and financial transformation occurs in increasingly and professionalized organizational societies.

Durkheim argued that the State can secure competent legislation only on general principles, and its massive and slow-moving machinery is ill-adapted to dealing with the highly specialized industrial activites and relations of the modern economies. As a result of this lack of adaptability of the State, there will be a constant oscillation between an excess of inexpert regulation and a condition of partial anarchy (cf. Barnes 1920).

Industrial transformation strategies and spatial development rely upon entrepreneurs in local economies who may 'hook onto' international trends. In the field of industrial and redistributive regional policy, the centralizing State model leads to inexpert regulation. This is, in itself, sufficient to block the aspired State coordination and control but (from the point of view of the State) the anarchic aspects of the situation are reinforced further: all programmes of regional policy will become embedded in local strategies for mobilizing resources from various State programmes, i.e., in the fields of housing, education, research etc. and these are uncoordinated at the centre. When this is so, institutions for which 'orderliness hinges upon centrality' cannot order selective policies efficiently.

Inexpert regulation and uncoordinated State programmes across policy fields also make the redistributive aims of regional policy uncertain. Such aims, however, were what motivated the use of the centralizing State model in the first place; the State was to overcompensate regions which were worse off than others in some respect. To work at all, various State programmes have become increasingly dependent on the skills of local intermediation structures mobilizing State programmes for local policies. Local intermediation skills are not necessarily situated in regions which are targeted for redistributive State programmes. And when intermediation structures perform well for entrepreneurs in local economies, State programmes are often coordinated from below, in a highly decentralized and creative fashion. An example is provided in the next section.

Local intermediaries: Responsiveness and democratic accountability[2]

The needs of small and medium sized enterprises (SMEs) increasingly came into political focus as, in the 1970s, governments began to view SMEs as job generators in otherwise weary Western economies. SMEs continue to command much interest from governments and the EU. Sometimes, however, it is not at all clear to an external observer whether the aims defined in public programmes respond more to political needs than to SMEs' needs. Hard-pressed governments need to be seen to be doing something to counter unemployment. Large firms lay off workers and, logically, small firms and entrepreneurs then come into focus.

In recent, methodologically reliable studies it seems that it is young rather than small firms that are net job-creators; but a firm's size and the hope that small will grow bigger, is still very much at the centre in the programme catalogues of governments. On top of this, the EU provides additional incentives to SMEs to grow. Do catalogues exist because SMEs have insistently demanded new programmes over the years? Not really. At least not as far as the programmes actually provided are concerned.

Several studies indicate that SMEs are largely unaware of the existence and detailed contents of the programmes available to them. When approached, they usually ask for more appropriate tax systems (especially for services), less red-tape, fewer legal restrictions on hiring and firing practices, etc. Selective State programmes are usually not high on SME lists. Hence, when discussing how if and how SMEs can be helped to grow, it is important that the relevance of public programmes targeted at firms is assessed from the point of view of SMEs and entrepreneurs. There are reasons to believe that, in many countries, officials have to apply programmes that are not adequately tested for SME relevance. Public administration has to be responsive to political aims as well as to target group needs. Political aims, as laid down in programme catalogues of the governments, reflect ambitions which are not necessarily conducive to the needs of SMEs; and especially not to the needs of firms in the service sectors of local economies. These are supposedly the sectors with prospects of job-creation in the future.

Given the catalogues of selective programmes now available in European States, responsiveness to entrepreneurs often implies a need to perform creatively locally, to organize intermediation structures that make programmes reach out. Creative local government activity increasingly helps to make programmes responsive to SMEs. However, State fundamentalists, who defend regional policy as their exclusive domain, provide local government with a good pretext for not having their involvement systematically reviewed within local democratic structures. Since regional policy is already coordinated locally, political as well as financial accountability for it is now diffuse.

The problems of political and administrative accountability created by intermediaries (entre preneurial local governments) are indeed real, if not necessarily problematic for SMEs. But the adherents of 'order by central government' cannot really avoid this 'partial anarchy'. The need for local intermediaries is a necessary result of the political ambitions of the centralizing State model. There are too many selective programmes in the public catalogues which have not had their significance for variegated local conditions tested. Local intermediaries have stepped in to create order according to local needs.

Intermediaries are of course (sometimes too) responsive to SMEs, as this is their raison d'être. To approach a situation where they are also responsive and accountable within democratic structures, several strategies are possible. One is to collapse groups of similiar programmes into more comprehensive schemes of wider scope. For central governments (and the EU) the consequence of this strategy would be to abandon high ambitions of selectivity and leave it to local governments to be responsible for 'fine-tuning'. If a wide range of programmes is to be retained in the public catalogues, each dealing with narrowly defined SME problems, it may be necessary to accept that the aimed-for selectivity, however strictly defined legally, can never be more than approximately attained. It follows that democratic accountability of policies will continue to be diffuse. States and EU cannot control implementation and local government need not take political responsibility.

In the SME policies basic to spatial development policies in Europe, the fuller range of strategic options for the relationship between programmes offered and employed, as well as SME problems covered, may be represented as:

	Public Programs Offered/Employed	
	Few broadly defined	Many narrowly defined
Number of SME Problems Covered		
Some	I	II
All	III	IV

The catalogues of public programmes in EU countries corresponds broadly to cell II of the Table. The situation occuring when effective intermediaries are at work is closer to cell III, however. Local intermediaries are professional enough to draw upon the many programmes offered, bundle them and use them to tackle all kinds of problems confronting SMEs. This suggests the seemingly paradoxical conclusion that creative implementation of programmes by local intermediaries may be more responsive to the needs of SMEs when there is little accountability as defined by objectives in government and EU programmes. If, on the other hand, intermediation were to be restrained in the interest of administrative accountability to central government and the EU, local development might well be slowed down with programme structures as they presently exist.

If, and this is a big if, creative local management of State or EU programmes is a way to help SMEs grow, more attention should be given to the local organization of accountable democratic intermediation structures, and less to the details of central government and EU programmes. Detailed specifications of public programmes, a trademark of the traditional centralizing State model, increases the necessity for creative local intermediation if a degree of responsiveness to SMEs is to be attained. To increase the chances for attaining a practical trade-off between responsive public programmes, democratic management and control of them, the role of local intermediation structures should be made more explicitly accountable to local government. In practice, in Sweden, this decentralized model already applies in regional policy which, by now, is but a small part of the development strategies of local government. Local government is already in charge, but the management and control strategies of the State lag behind. They conform more to the centralizing State model that by now is at variance with the common knowledge of how 'things are done'. This is the reason why the concept 'local industrial policy' (LIP) is suggested here, namely, to signal that rather dramatic shifts have taken place within the set of actors of spatial development policy.

Among firms (especially SMEs) and local government, State 'regional policy' has lost credi- bility in past decades. In the same period of time, however, 'region' and 'regionalization' have evolved into politically correct catchwords on the EU circuit of scholars, consultants, administrators and politicians. Is it just coincidence that 'spatial development policy' and catchwords, such as 'Europe of the regions' and 'European regionalization', have come to the fore concurrently with the struggle of European welfare States? We surmise it is not. These slogans still entail, on inspection, much of the notion, favoured by representatives of l'ancien régimes, 'that orderliness hinges upon centrality', albeit focused on Brussels and Strasbourg rather than on national capitals. The results, however, of efforts in past decades to change the geography of Europe's basic industrial structures by regional or other spatial policies are hardly discernable. In thirty years, regional policy seems to have created few new bases for sustained economic growth and job-creation in Europe. Successful entrepreneurs seem not to gather in spaces where States want economic development.

In response to inexpert State policy: Local Industrial Policy[3]

In the complex of modern economies, political centres, including the European Union's, lack theories to effectively support 'local' economies which, in effect, may be hooked onto global trends out of the control of central governments. Lacking theoretic foundations, the politically motivated selective regional policies of 20th century l'ancien regimes are mixtures of inexpert regulation, from the point of view of entrepreneurs and local government, and partial anarchy from the point of view of State and EU programme accountability. Durkheim's observation a hundred years ago seems prescient.

There are 287 municipalities in Sweden. In 1987, a government commission identified some 515 'resource centres' throughout the country; mainly non-profit organizations established to provide some kind of technical competence to qualify (aspiring) entrepreneurs, firms and post-secondary school students. Most centres had been established since 1980. To non-Swedes, the flurry of local activity to establish local resource centres throughout the 1980s and continuing into the early 1990s, may lead observers to the conclusion that, surely, in centralized Sweden, this surge must be due to a new State policy. Such a conclusion would be in line with the proverbial centralizing State model of Sweden, but it overlooks the politico-administrative changes that have evolved in the local/central set-up of 'regional' policy.[4]

Swedish regional policy commenced as an extension of selective labour market policy. In the political agenda, if not in practice, throughout the 1970s and 80s, regional policy became more and more decoupled from labour market policy, and oriented towards creating jobs rather than reducing unemployment. Policy aims changed from an emphasis on State regional planning to an intra-regional focus, and from the central State as the arbiter of economic development to county agencies as coordinators of the regional policy instruments of the State. However, the reorientation, effective from the late 1970s, refers more to the agenda of county and (some national) State agencies than to the 'regional' policy in which they were actually partners in implementing. Because meanwhile the role of municipalities had begun to grow significantly, regional policy had started to develop into local industrial policy, that is, the practice that local governments embed State policies in their own strategies of development. From the early 1990s on, State agencies began to be embedded to a much greater extent than before in municipal strategies of economic development; sometimes in 'regions' created by local governments, amd crossing county and even national borders.

Swedish municipalities have rapidly increased their competence in the industrial policy field. The increased involvement of local governments in industrial policy formation ensued partly from a need to respond to the often uncoordinated schemes of several national boards and their regional agencies, i.e., to help coordinate State and EU programmes 'from below' as it were. Municipal resources for local industrial policy (LIP), measured as the number of full time employees in the field, increased more than four times from 1982 to 1994, and even more in those parts of Sweden where State agencies have larger budgets for regional development and to where EU funds are primarily targeted. However, differences in LIP, in staff, organization and commitment decreased rapidly across Swedish municipalities throughout the last decade. Concurrently with these developments, State agencies have had sharp reductions of staff in the regional policy field.

As a consequence of these 'trends', starting in the 1980s, shortcomings have become visible in Sweden in the programmematic, organizational and constitutional division of labour between central and local government with regard to spatial development policy. The transformation process towards local industrial policy continues to manifest itself, but it is still not clear what the consequences will be for the Swedish l'ancien régime. It is clear, however, that municipalities act as if the industrial policy monopoly of the State were withering.

Until recently, industrial policy was considered a State preserve in Sweden. According to State reviews, municipalities lacked the overview, legal competence and resources to participate, if at all, as little else than executors of State policy in the field. Several arguments were used against a greater involvement of municipalities in industrial policy. Legalists referred to the Municipal Act that narrowly bounds the role of local government in industrial policy. Industry lobbies feared unfair competition practices if municipalities engaged themselves actively; and State agencies argued that municipalities would endanger systematic State intervention in the economy if their role increased in industrial policy. Fears of unfair competition proved to be exaggerated; special legislation exists to remedy the problem, and over the in past decades few cases have been filed. Fears that systematic State intervention might become more difficult are academic; industrial policy such intervention is hard to find in the first place.

The legal arguments against local industrial policy proved to be largely beside the point, the potential for greater municipal involvement is large enough within the existing legal frame- work. Besides, in past decades, State-induced legal changes, outside industrial policy proper but with direct consequences for it, have made it hard for local government not to engage actively in the policy field. Legal restrictions or not, citizens do expect that municipalities actively help create jobs; local elections are contested on this issue, especially in parts of Sweden where employment is the main problem since the 1970s. There are important political factors behind the greater involvement of Swedish municipalities in industrial policy.

National politics have proved ineffective. Municipalities cannot take a back-seat position any longer and simply tell citizens to wait till the State or EU gets its act together. Meanwhile few citizens expect much neither from the State nor the European Union.

Swedish municipalities do not, however, conceive local industrial policy in terms of a 'zero-sum game'. That their tasks have increased is not taken to mean that other actors are unimportant. There is scope for more efforts by all interested parties, but municipalities cannot avoid any longer coordinating the mobilization of resources. They see various regional State agencies as very important for the developments of LIP; but only one municipality out of four claims that central government is very important. Three municipalities out of four view local firms as very important in their formation of LIP (Hjern 1992). A new, more market-oriented than State

oriented model of LIP is being formed in Sweden (Svenska kommunförbundet 1996).

To sum up, from the 1980s onwards, the coordination of Swedish
spatial development policy has started to evolve along a decentralizing
State model, i.e.,local industrial policy. But so far this has come about by
default rather than by the insights suggested by Durkheim's prescient observation on the limited chances of success when States try to structure
local economies by statutes and selective programmes. Industrial policy is
one of the few remaining policies in Sweden for which the virtues and
(economic) efficiency of decentralized organisation is still not very much
praised by central government. In practice, however, processes towards
local industrial policy are manifest. Hence, the model of the centralizing
State is kept formally in a policy area for which it was counterproductive in
the first place.

Local Industrial Policy: A challenge for European l'ancien régimes

To start developing democratic and administrative accountability structures
systematically in spatial development policy, the role of local government
needs to be acknowledged and defined. This requires discussions on a new
division of labour between central and local governments in a policy field
that central governments until recently considered its own pre- rogative. A
new division of labour is, de facto, being institutionalized. Innovative development in economics and politics usually start from below. L'ancien
régimes do not change until their institutions are manifestly sidetracked. If
the Swedish case is germane to Europe, this situation is rapidly approach-
ing in the Europe of 'lancien régimes, i.e., the EU.

In several European countries local-central relationships have out-
grown their traditional constitutional, political and financial setups.[5] This
has little to do with recent EU developments, but analysts of the spatial
development policy of the union will have to take systematically into consideration that the political élites of member States for a long time have
had political and economic problems with their version of 'the modern
project', the centralizing State model that peaked in the 1980s with the
social welfare State.

Unfortunately mainstream theories of European spatial development policy cling to the idea that the continuation of the modern project

depends on the existing centrality of individual States and, post Maastricht, of the EU.[6] In economic models 'regions' have been introduced as the focus of attention but the space is seldomly defined with other criteria than the ones used to depict subnational administrative units of States. While this may be statistically convenient, it seems less evident why theories of economic development should be bounded by boundaries of administration.

To quite an extent recent 'regionalization' processes in Europe occur because administrative boundaries of States have proved to be incapacitating for local strategies to attain economic development. Firms, in democratic societies, usually do not mould their behaviour according to the administrative regions of States. So to the extent that scholars are interested in 'regionalization' as part of 'new' spatial development processes in Europe it would seem necessary to keep track of sub-regional activities, and actors participating significantly in these. The slogan, 'Europe of the regions', should be changed to 'regionalization of local activities in Europe' to help increase the relevance of studies of European spatial development policies. It would mean to approach spatial development more through the rationales of local actors than most research in the field is designed to do. It does not mean, however, that other actors or non-local resources should not be included in studies. But to be efficient in economic development in the long run these have to form part of sustained local strategies. If such strategies do not exist 'external' resources more likely than not are wasted as far as economic development is concerned. But short-term, again and again, they may, if Swedish experiences of past decades are possible to generalize, fulfill political needs of symbolic redistributive politics.

This is where a connex exists between spatial economic development policies and local democracy. Sustained local strategies of development will not ensue if accountability of the changing, often politically opportunistic, programme catalogues of 'regional' policy is left with the bureacracy of States, even if subnational. It is responsible to States (and EU) which cannot coordinate all policies that in practice pertain to spatial development. There is no way that citizens as voters could ensure democratic accountability from the bureacracy or the policy makers of States (or EU), even if political party systems functioned well in European States - and they do not.

To have sustained local strategies of development evolve democratic accountability will have to be organized more clearly by local government. Local governments that create no sustained strategies of economic development should be possible to be held accountable by voters in elections, meaning that local political parties will have to engage in discussions with the population on their own merits and with their own ideas (that need not be exclusively their own). Since most other policies that correlate with spatial development need the attention and plans of local government it seems unlikely that 'regional' policy of economic growth will form without the democratic accountability of local governments, sometimes in cooperation with each other, i.e. through 'regionalization' of local industrial policy (LIP). Municipalities in Sweden have started to move from traditional 'regional policy' towards LIP, but has the Swedish State or EU? In one important respect it has not. In spatial development policies neither the Swedish State nor EU supports the 'free' municipalities that is needed to regenerate democracy in European l'ancien régimes.

The argument of this article is that qua 'regional policy' spatial development policies in Europe cling to the centralizing State model of recent welfare States. By not explicitly adopting the 'local industrial policy' concepts European States and EU pursue counterproductive strategies, democratic accountability and local economic development is not focused in combination and States cannot systematically take responsibility for the latter through resdistributive policies of the past. Mixed economies would not function without some public intervention, however appropriate are calls for deregulation. In spatial development policies, the centralizing State model is overextended and (redistributively) even counterproductive.

State intervention and services for spatial development is based on structuring by statute and selective programmes. Without local intermediation programmes cannot be adapted to the specialized, organizational and financial processes of modern mixed economies. Already Durkheim foresaw the oscillation between an excess of inexpert regulation and a condition of partial anarchy of control that would ensue from the centralizing State. He proposes more attention to local intermediation structures to remedy the situation. His analysis seems entirely modern against the cases of research presented in the article.

Dissatisfied with central government schemes, local governments have started effectively to decentralize spatial development policies and to 'regionalize' it. But inexpert legal structuring and creative implementation of State programmes by local intermediaries that organize outside democratic accountability structures have rendered spatial development policies unpredictable, both from the point of view of economic theories of resource allocation as well as from democratic theories of State leadership and political control. The institutional assumptions of economic theories, also in regional economics, are too crude to help define a basis of reform in the direction of local industrial policy. And democratic theory in Europe is set in the national history of centralizing welfare States.

A scenario for spatial development policies qua local industrial policy may draw upon features already practiced in the emergent policy field. As pieces of research on SME policy demonstrates, the more selective the State programmes, the less likely it is to ensure democratic accountability and responsiveness to SMEs by State administration alone. To increase chances to attain a practical trade-off between responsive public programmes and democratic accountability, the number of programmes should be cut and the role of intermediation structures be more explicitly controlled by local government.

As the 'resource centre movement' in Sweden and elsewhere demonstrates, State regional policy instruments was not adequately adjusted to the need for increasing investments in human capital manifesting itself in the 1980s. But local governments, together with firms, even in proverbially centralistic Sweden, initiated local strategies to improve regional qualification structures. With creative 'multi-pocket budgeting' practices that made use of resources from firms and several national boards responsible for sectoral policies. This case provides additional insights of the reasons why redistributive State regional policy fail to help the formation of more clearly defined local industrial policy agendas. This could be summarized in four points:

1. **Politically**, sectors policies have made deep inroads on and contained redistributive regional policy proper. Job-creation is a process of combining several sector policies in a spatial frame. EU and central governments has little capability to overview the process.
2. **Administratively**, decentralization of tasks have ensued, coordinated from below as local actors increasingly have invested in competence to define and mobilize publicand and private resources for their challenges.
3. **Empirically**, the effects of regional policy instruments have been hard to establish.
4. **Theoretically**, received growth centre and planning notions have lost momentum and key concepts, such as 'region' and 'branch' of the economy, are under review.

European spatial development policies qua local industrial policy should entail a reduction of the number of detailed and standardized State and EU programmes, a minimum of EU and State redistributive proclamations and support to the formation of local agendas to start to restore democratic accountability in the field. In practice, the coordination of (successful) strategies in the field already ensues locally, but the States (or EU) still claim a role as arbiter of development which it is not able to fullfill predictibly. The State is stymied by its incapacity to effectively coordinate selective programmes across policy fields. Local governments coordinate programmes 'from below' but need not bear full political responsibility for results in the industrial policy field as long as the centralizing State model commands the interests of policy makers and analysts.

Local government should be the basic unit democratically accountable for spatial development policy. If needed, 'regionalization' should ensue from local government coordination. There is no logical reasons why political local parties should not win elections with convincing, differentiated strategic alliances for industrial policies between networks of municipalities. Accountability in the public domain unfolds in conjunction with democratic development. Since regional democracy is presently not a salient feature on European territory, however 'region' is defined, democratic political orders, EU, State or regional, need be based in a local presence. Ideologically 20th century l'ancien régimes have retained this idea but do not practice it. Constitutional antecedents of regional democracy, possibly with the exception of national regions (developing into States?) like in Belgium, are few in Europe, but local government is an established form constitutionally. A revival of local democracy is necessary (but not sufficient) for European democracy to become but a slogan.

In conclusion, spatial development policy should be structured, as suggested by recent Swedish experiences, to make local government increasingly accountable for a small number of broad State programmes, without redistributive aims, mainly concerned with qualification strategies, while central government, in line with Durkheims suggestions before the period of welfare State hubris, retain accountability for enacting a few competent general principles of industrial policy. The latter could in due time be elevated to EU heights, while the detailed formation of strategies of qualification would be as misplaced there as with central governments.

Notes

1   Some factors explaining developments from regional policy towards local industrial policy are discussed by Ewers 1987: 339ff in the setting of the Federal Repulic of Germany. More generally by Reese 1993, Bates 1995, Walzer 1995 and Pierre 1997. In the the Scandinavian setting the trend is discussed by nordREFO 1982, Fredriksson 1984:175ff and Grahm

       1988. Also, cf. Hjern 1989a, 1990 and 1996 as well as Olson 1995 and Pi-
       erre 1995.

2   This section is an updated version of a paper first prepared by the author
       for an OECD report 1989. It draws upon materials from C. Hull & B.
       Hjern 1987, and Hjern 1990. Recent developments, including, EU pro-
       grammes for Sweden have not changed the relevance of the empirical
       analysis (cf. Hanberger 1991, Carlsson 1993 and Olson 1995).

3   Data in this section are from surveys by the author on all Swedish munici-
       palities (apart from the three big cities) in 1985, 1988 and 1991. Results
       are presented in Hjern 1987, Hjern 1988, Hjern 1989a and 1992. Materials
       from a 1994 survey have been available to check trends (cf. Pierre 1995).

4   In an assessment 1988 of "Regional policy as a distinctive field" in the
       Nordic countries, "the lag of the policy behind actual needs will become
       the recurring topic of the discussion" (Oscarsson 1988:14). The same
       author, a central government policy strategist, claims that the need for re-
       thinking regional policy is even more necessary as a result of the financial
       crisis of the welfare State (Oscarsson 1994:117). Apart from an adaptation
       to EU programme structures, much rethinking by central government can-
       not be reported, however.

5   The literature is by now rather large on this topic. With regard to local
       government, States and the EU, interesting discussions may be found in
       Bache 1992, Hoffschulte 1994, Loughlin 1994, Mabileau 1994, Rhodes
       1991, Toonen 1993 and Weiss 1992.

6   But cf. Beck 1994, Kitzmueller 1994, Touraine 1992 and Willke 1992.

References

Andersson, R. and A. Malmberg (1988), Regional Struktur och industriella strate-
    gier Norden (Regional Structure and Industrial Strategies in the Nordic
    Countries). Nordrefo.

Bache, I. (1992), Bypassing the centre? Assessing the value of UK local govern-
    ment participating in European transnational coalitions. MA thesis. Uni-
    versity of Sheffield, Department of Politics.

Barnes, H. F. (1920), 'Durkheim's Contribution to the Reconstruction of Political
    Theory', Political Science Quartely, 1920: 236-254.

Beck, U. (1993), Die Erfindung des Politischen. Frankfurt a. M.

Carlsson, L. (1993), Samhällets oreglerbarhet (The ungovernability of society).
    Sympsion Graduale.

Durkheim, E. (1964), The Division of Labor in Society, London: MacMillan.

Ewers, H.-J. (1987), 'Zur Dezentralisierung der Industripolitik' in M. Fritsch & C.
    Hull (eds), Arbeitsplatzdynamik und Regionalentwicklung. Berlin: Edition
    Sigman.

Fredriksson, C. (1984), 'Från industribunden regionalpolitik till ortsbunden indus-
    tripolitik'. nordREFO 1984:1-2.

Grahm, L. (1988), Att välja regionalpolitik. NordREFO: Nordstedts Tryckeri AB.

Hanberger, A. (1991), Lokalt samarbete och global integration (Local cooperation and globalization). Research report. Umeå university, Department of Political Science.

Harding, A. (1996), Regional Government in Britain: An Economic Solution? Policy Press.

Häussl, R. (1994), 'Föderalismus darf nicht vor Gemeinden halt machen', Österreich Kommunal 1994/1, p. 12-13.

Hjern, B. (1987), Kommunal näringspolitik - ansvar och kompetens. Stockholm: The Swedish Association of Local Authorities (ISBN 91-7344-696-3).

Hjern, B. (1988), 'Centralstatlig avreglering för lokal näringslivsutveckling'. nordREFO 1988: 126-154.

Hjern, B. (1989a), Kommunal näringspolitik: professionalisering och demokratisering. Stockholm: Swedish Association of Local Authorities.

Hjern, B. (1989b),, 'Decentralized Sweden' in D. Ashford (Ed.), Discretionary politics. 1989 Yearbook: International Review of Comparative Public Policy.

Hjern, B. (1989c), 'Improvement of Regional Qualification Structures as a Task of Regional Economic Policies'. Paper preparted for the 5th International Conference on 'Innovation and Regional Development', Berlin, 1-2 December 1988. Forthcoming 1989 in the Proceedings of the conference.

Hjern, B. (1990), 'Industrial Policy: The Demise of the Centralizing State Model'. nordREFO 1990:6, Academic Press - Copenhagen.

Hjern, B. (1992),'Illegitimate Democracy: A Case for Multiorganizational Policy Analysis'. Policy Currents 1992:1.

Hjern, B. (1995), Självförvaltning eller lokal demokrati (Local government as state administrative or local democratic units). Svenska kommunförbundet 1995.

Hjern, B. (1996), 'Lokal mångfald som kaos eller demokratisk fördjupning' (Local variety as chaos or democratic regeneration) in H. Månsson Med periferin i centrum. Glesbygdsverkets skriftserie 2.

Hoffschulte, H. (1994), 'Kommunale und regionale Selbstverwaltung in Europa der Regionen - Zur Rolle der vierten Ebene in der EU'. F.-L .Knemeyer, Europa der Regionen - Europa der Kommunen. Nomos Verlagsgesellschaft.

Hogwood, B. (1996), In search of community identity. York Publishing Services.

Hull, C and B. Hjern (1987), Helping Small Firms Grow: An Implementation Approach. Beckenham: Croom Helm.

Johansson, B. (1993), Ekonomisk Dynamik i Europa (Economic Dynamics in Europe). Liber-Hermods Malmö.

Kitzmueller, E. (1994), 'Europa - aber welcher Typ von Moderne?' Österreichische Zeitschrift fuer Politikwissensschaft, 1994:1.

Knemeyer, F.-L. (1994), Europa der Regionen - Europa der Kommunen. Nomos Verlagsgesellschaft.

Leijonhufvud, A. (1981), Information and Control: Essays in Macro-Economic Theory. New York: Oxford University Press.

Loughlin, M. (1994), The constitutional status of Local government. CLD Research Report 3.

Luhman, N. (1982), The Differentiation of Society. Columbia University Press, New York. (Translation from German by S. Holmes and C. Larmore).

Mabileau, A. (1996), Kommunalpoltik und -verwaltung in Frankreich: Das 'lokala System' Frankreichs. Birkhäuser Verlag.

Nilsson, J.-E. (1995), Sverige i förnyelsens Europa (Sweden in a rebounding Europe). Liber-Hermods Malmö.

NordREFO (1982), Lokal näringspolitik. Oslo: Universitetsförlaget.

Olsson, J. (1995), Den lokala näringspolitikens politiska ekonomi (The Political Economy of Local Industrial Policy). Örebro Studies 12: Högskolan i Örebro.

Oscarsson, G. (1988), 'Sammanfattande analys och förslag till fortsatt forskning' in nordREFO, Om regionalpolitiken som politikområde. Helsinki: Painokaari op.

Oscarsson, G. (1994), 'Vilken regionalpolitik får vi efter solskenspolitikernas uttåg?' (Which regional policy after the demise of sunny side politicians). nordREFO 1994:5. Rounborgs grafiske hus, Holstebro Danmark.

Pierre, J. (1995), 'When The Going Gets Tough: Changing Local Economic Development Strategies in Sweden', in N. Walzer (1995), Local Economic Development: Incentives and International Trends. Westview Press.

Pierre, J. (1997), Partnerships in Urban Governance: European and American Experiences. Houndmills, Basingstoke: Macmillan Publishers Ltd.

Reese, L. (1993), 'Decision Rules in Local Economic Development', Urban Affairs Quartely, vol. 28:501-513.

Rhodes, R.A.W. (1991), 'Now Nobody Understands the System: The Changing Face of Local Government' i P. Norton, New Directions in British Politics? Aldershot: Edward Elgar.

Svenska kommunförbundet (1996), Framgångsrika kommuner - mot en ny näringspolitisk model? (Succesful municipalities - towards a new model of industrial policy?). Report, Swedish Association of Municipalities.

Toonen, T. (1993), A 'Country without Regions' and the Committee of the Regions: The Case of the Netherlands. Research report. University of Leiden, Department of Public Administration.

Touraine, A. (1992), Critique de la modernité. Paris.

Walzer, N. (1995), Local Economic Development: Incentives and International Trends. Westview Press.

Weiss, J. (1992), 'Föderalismus - Bilanz und Vorschau'. Östereichische Monatshefte 92:1-2.

Willke, H. (1992), Ironie des States: Grundlinien einer Staatstheorie polizentrischer Gesellschaft. Frankfurt a.M.

Wittrock, B. (1988), 'Rise and Development of the Modern State: Democracy in Context' in Democracy, State and Justice: Critical Perspectives and New Interpretations, Stockhom: Almqvist & Wiksell International.

Discussion by: Michael Spindelegger

First of all, thank you for the invitation to this workshop on 'Desiderata for further development of European town and country planning policies' at the Austrian Academy of Sciences. When the former Minister, Mr. Jürgen Weiss, asked me two weeks ago to stand in, I had no idea the audience would be so international and prestigious. I am sure you will understand that my comments cannot rival with Professor Hjern's excellent lecture. For that reason I will try to touch upon different aspects of European regional policy from an Austrian point of view.

First of all let me introduce myself. At the moment I am a member of the Austrian People's Party delegation in the European Parliament. After graduating in law at Vienna University, I worked in the regional administration of Lower Austria, where I acquired practical experience in town and country planning. When I became a member of the Austrian Federal Council (Bundesrat) in 1992, I worked in banking. In the European Parliament I am now a member of the committee for economic and monetary affairs and industrial policy.

Professor Hjern has compared the representatives of centralistic democracies, now meeting in Brussels and Strasbourg, with their 19th century counterparts who met in Vienna in 1814-1815. At this meeting in Vienna today, be it only because of my age, I hope to be one of the exceptions Professor Hjern admitted exist. Fortunately, in Brussels and Strasbourg nowadays, you do not meet only centralists, and I would like to cite Article 3b of the Treaty of Maastricht to convey my first impressions of the European Union:

> *'In areas which do not fall within its exclusive competence, the Community shall take action, in accordance with the principle of subsidiarity, only if, and in so far as, the objectives of the proposed action cannot be sufficiently achieved by the Member States and can therefore, by reasons of the scale on effects of the proposed action, be better achieved by the Community'.*

This hardly sounds like a constitution for a centralistic Community.

In Austria we have less experience with European town and country planning policies in practice, being, as people say in Brussels, one of the European Union's youngest members. The same holds true for Sweden and Finland. In general, the experience we do have may be considered as positive, especially in comparison with the national achievements of Austrian town and country planning policy.

Let me give you some examples to justify this view:

1. To be translated into action, all town and country planning policies need people and, of course, money. In Lower Austria alone, the amount of funds for objectives 2 and 5b, from 1995 to 1999, is about 1.8 billion ATS. A further 1.8 billion of Austrian contributions - from both the Federal and from the Lower Austrian Governments - will make a wide range of intensive measures possible. The EU's structural funds in particular will influence the rates of public investment in specific areas eligible for assistance.
2. The EU's structural funds are used for specific projects, but these projects cannot be seen as isolated investments. The elimination of the structural weakness of a whole region is the objective. Thus, the structural fund regulations have made it necessary to introduce a rational and consistent process of planning and evaluating public investment. The selection of major investment projects is subject to intense scrutiny - not only by the national government ministries but also by regional representatives and by the European Union.
3. In Lower Austria we have four so-called 'regional managers'. They travel throughout their designated parts of Lower Austria, and every local politician tries to convince them that all investments should be made in his locality. It is the duty of these regional managers to support regional activities. The European Commission is only competent to confirm Lower Austria's general programme for the regeneration of less developed regions. Decisions on particular projects are made by the regional Lower Austrian government.

I am not speaking in defence of centralism: I simply believe that town and country planning is - as the constitution of the European Union says - partly 'an action which cannot be sufficiently achieved by the Member States'.

Let me now give you a short survey of regional economic incentives.

Government expenditure of all Member States taken together in the form of regional financial incentives was running in the second half of the 1980s at 7.7 billion ECU per year, with a further 2 billion ECU devoted to tax incentives. This amounts to about 30 ECU per year/per capita across the EU as a whole, or about 90 ECU per capita in the less privileged regions. Unfortunately, I do not have the latest figures, but this shows the force of regional economic incentives.

Expenditure on regional policy by Austria takes into account respective regional needs, and so assistance tends to go to those regions in greatest need. Burgenland, as an objective 1 area, is proof that the Austrian Government has not reduced its own structural expenditure. The same holds true for the objective 2 and 5b areas in Austria. As I said before, the EU's structural funds, in particular, will influence the rate of public investment in specific areas eligible for assistance. Today, the problem of assessing 'additionality' is solved, and the precise level of contributions made by the EU to specific objectives is quantifiable.

In the 1960s and 1970s, regional policy financial incentives were concentrated on the manufacturing sector. At that time manufacturing was the dominant sector which exported from the region and hence was the sector on which most of the service sector depended. In the 1980s the situation changed. Much of the traditional manufacturing sector ceased to expand, at least in terms of employment, and some industries have experienced a long-term structural decline in employment. At the same time new manufacturing industries, based heavily on research and development and highly qualified staff, have grown rapidly. There has also been rapid growth in services. Tourism, in particular, is still important for Austria.

Under these circumstances the efficiency of regional policy will be enhanced to the extent that it is directed less at traditional manufacturing industries and more towards newer R&D related enterprises and, important for Austria, towards tourism and business-service activities. Although Austria was not a member of the EU during these changes, our economy has adapted to those new circumstances reasonably quickly. Austria has moved towards recognising the important role of services in the process of modern regional development and has adapted its regional policy accordingly.

The question as to whether the adjustment of national infrastructure programmes for regional policy reasons represent an efficient use of regional policy resources is complex. In the short run the answer is often 'no'; but in the medium and long run the answer has to be a qualified 'yes'. In the long run the provision of infrastructure facilities is a necessary condition for the successful economic development of the less privileged regions.

Ultimately, the success of the structural funds will be measured by the progress made by the recipients towards independence, i.e., the development of an economy which is internationally competitive and which permits a standard of living close to the Austrian average without further transfers from wealthier regions. Some experts argue that the policy of seeking improvements in the productive capacity of an economy by offering financial assistance for public investment is self-defeating and can never succeed in narrowing the gap. This is because regions in receipt of financial aid adjust their habits to the new situation, become dependent on the financial inflows, and then fail to develop those productive activities which would permit financial independence. I should beg to differ.

Narrowing the gap is the aim we should reach within the next decades. Let me now turn to the steps necessary for this economic and social objective.

If regions want to be more important and influential in future, co-operation and coordination between them must improve. Nowadays, in Austria, there are only a few regions with their own specific identity. Even in the east of Austria people do not have a deep feeling for the region they live in. Yet a specific identity is a precondition for development. As Professor Hjern said, the basic power of effective action for regional development processes lies with the local actors. He demonstrated this for Sweden. The same holds true for Austria. On the other hand, the question arises as to whether national States will accept such processes. Let me remind you of the Italian reaction to having only one office in Brussels for both North and South Tyrolean affairs.

In general the EU reflects the interests and political will of all its members. Like everything, the European Union has both advantages and disadvantages. Whatever the future may hold, it is to be hoped that the European Union will continue to be the guarantor of the peaceful development of European regions.

Thank you for your attention.

5 New Dimensions to Regional Theory and Policy in the European Union

STUART HOLLAND

The Scope and Limits of Traditional Policies

Traditional regional policies have tended to assume interregional mobility of both capital and labour. Such a model implied that capital would flow to areas of lower labour costs, and labour would flow inversely to more developed areas and where labour is scarce. The further implication was that factor proportions and rates of return would be equalized by such mobility.

Such policies also have assumed that reducing production costs in less advanced areas would offset lower efficiency and thereby equalize competitive conditions. This was the rationale behind regional development grants or incentives which either would increase profits and investible funds for firms in less developed regions, or equalize a 'normal' profit for firms in different regions.

A further assumption of such policies was that such regional incentives would attract investment by firms from other regions. In this sense it implied a transfer of investment and thus modernisation from the centre *to* the periphery.

This was combined with the argument that backward agricultural regions should be industrialized, and that industrial investment should be concentrated in growth centres or development *pôles*. Inspired by the reasoning of Francois Perroux, these would exploit external economies in the widest sense and attract further resources.[1]

A range of indirect incentives and direct measures, including loans, grants, tax relief and lower interest rates, were adopted by different governments to fulfil this strategy.

While the best of such policies worked with some effect in their time, they were appropriate to the era of national mass production. They are less appropriate or ineffective in an era of multinational and increasingly flexible production.

Towards a New Policy Framework

Whatever the historical judgement on traditional policies, it is evident that they need to be transcended in a new era by a new policy framework.

As implied by Tables 1 and 2, this needs to:

1. Respond to the needs and issues arising from both the new internal market and the intense globalisation of the world economy;
2. *Adjust to an era in which investment, production and trade is dominated by multinational big business*;
3. Recognise that comparative interregional cost advantages within the European Union will not be sufficient for enterprise in less developed regions (LDRs) to compete on cost alone with either the more developed regions (MDRs) or the emergent industrializing economies of Asia;
4. Assist innovation and diversification to offset declining employment in hitherto strongly industrialized (Objective 2) areas;
5. Encourage firms to do so by projecting a joint innovation trajectory with related firms *rather than relying on traditional cost-based external economies as well as to adapt to new methods of work organization on the lines of Japanese flexible or lean production;*
6. *Learn from the symbiotic public/private cooperation of the Developmental State or Relational State or Networked State model which has proved so successful in Japan, South Korea and elsewhere in Asia;*
7. *Recognise that the self-adjustment of factor proportions implicit in the traditional model no longer obtains because net EC interregional migration has virtually ceased;*
8. Take account of the fact that the increase of international migration into the Union tends to be to more rather than less developed areas;
9. Realise that multinational firms tend to locate in central or intermediate regions rather than less or least developed areas.

In particular, the new policy framework needs to:

1. *Promote endogenous and self-sustaining development* in either peripheral or less favoured regions and areas;
2. Achieve more balanced development of both industry and services rather than focus on industry and industrial growth centres;
3. *Provide soft infrastructure in modern business services* rather than focus on industry and industrial growth centres;
4. Assist medium-sized firms through multiregional or interregional networking in such a way as to gain some of the features of multinational companies, without needing to become large firms.

Table 5.1 Traditional and New Regional Policies

Traditional Regional Policies	New Regional Policies
Hypothesis	**Hypothesis**
Interregional flows of labour and interregional capital flows	Immobility of interregional labour International flows of capital and labour
Problems	**Problems**
Lack of qualified labour	Lack of qualified labour *and* entrepreneurship
Lack of capital	Lack of process and product innovation
Inadequate economies of scale	Inadequate economies of scope
Strategy	**Strategy**
Spatial concentration in Growth Poles or Centres	Interregional networking
Compensate for lack of competitiveness	Increase regional competitiveness
Financial transfers to firms and regions	Income transfers to weakest social groups
Exploit unequal wage costs	Align minimum wages
Key Development Factors	**Key Development Factors**
Offset barriers to entry	Overcome barriers to entry and expansion
Re-locate centre firm investment to periphery	Promote and reinforce entrepreneurship
Promote industrial development	Promote multi-sectoral development
Objectives	**Objectives**
Reduce production costs	Flexible production and distribution
Offset unequal development	Offset both unequal endowment and unequal competition
Instruments	**Instruments**
Subsidies to industrial firms	Improve producer services
General incentives	Specific incentives
Increase hard infrastructure	Increase soft infrastructure
Focus on interregional development	Focus on interregional development agencies and interregional networking
Interregional credit agencies and financial agencies	Increased Community role in financial transfers
Regional agreements on location with national firms	Regional Development Agreements/Strategic Plans

Traditional Regional Policies	New Regional Policies
Effects	**Effects**
Increasing dependence	Increased independence
Limits to competitiveness	Increased competitiveness
Conflict with competition policy	Broader compatibility with competition policy

Source: Stuart Holland, *The European Imperatives: Economic and Social Cohesion in the 1990s,* 1992 Report to Commission President Jacques Delors and Commissioners Bangemann, Papandreou and Millan, published by Spokesman Books, Nottingham, 1993.

Table 5.2 Comparision of Frameworks

The National Regional Framework	Complementary Community Framework
Development Model	**Development Model**
Economic development is promoted by the interdependence between endogenous and exogenous actors	Innovation and competitiveness is promoted by interregional networks and interregional cooperation
Spatial Framework	**Spatial Framework**
National problem regions	Networks of EC and non-EC regions
Policy Strategy	**Policy Strategy**
Integrated sectoral and regional programmes	Tackle common European problems
Partnership between local actors	Promote interregional cooperation
Promote local entrepreneurship	Decrease transaction costs in interregional relations
Policy Design	**Policy Design**
Mainly centre to periphery	Both centre and periphery
Regions and local authorities elaborate Strategic Plans	EC evaluates specific projects in relation to the Strategic Plans
	EC evaluates and decides on project proposals

The National Regional Framework	Complementary Community Framework
Financing	**Financing**
Central transfers to problem regions	Complementary EC financing role
Coordination of regional and national programmes	Interregional cooperation
Consistency and transparency	Consistency and transparency
Institutional Procedures	**Institutional Procedures**
Hierarchical principle	Subsidiarity principle
Vertical coordination between regions, local government and Member States	Horizontal cooperation between regions
Relations Between Regional and Non-Regional Policies	**Relations Between Regional and Non-Regional Policies**
Regional policy aims for national cohesion	Regional policy aims for Community cohesion
Policy mediates different and often conflicting objectives	Policies aim to reinforce common and complementary objectives

Source: Stuart Holland, The European Imperative. ibid.

1. Through networking as joint innovation and marketing transcend centre to periphery policies by policies of centre with periphery;
2. Thereby help offset the dynamics of unequal competition between bigger medium-sized and small-sized business.

The Dynamics of Unequal Competition

The basic imperative for small and medium-sized firms is first of all to survive and secondly — if possible — to grow. Undoubtedly, location plays a part in qualifying chances for survival and growth in the small and medium enterprise sector. Nonetheless, a major threat to survival and the main barrier to growth for SMEs is not location, but unequal competition from bigger business.

> *The threat was evident in the expectation of the Cecchini analysis that gains in the single market for larger firms would mean '... the disappearance of the smallest or least efficient companies, or their concentration, and the development of new and greater specialisation'.*[2]

> *The problem with this analysis is that it is not only the least efficient small firms but also the most efficient which may disappear in the new internal market.*

For instance, a large multi-divisional multinational company seeking to enter a new market may face some problems of management coordination in the process; but it will not also face the problem of moving from owner-entrepreneurship to a multidivisional structure. A smaller firm may well do so, and thus face not only

1. Innovation costs in developing a new product or market area, but also
2. Organization costs in trying to expand its managerial capacity to meet the scale or geographical spread of market demand for its new product.

Thus the successful small firm may find itself penalised by success, whereas the successful larger firm may simply profit from its penalties by taking over its market share.

This is suggested, inter alia, from the findings of Storey et al [1987] in a survey of both UK and West German data that:

> *those (small) businesses which were growing the fastest encountered the most problems. It is characteristic that of those new firms starting in business perhaps half will cease to trade within three years, and the vast majority of those which remain in business will have ceased to exhibit any increase in employment once they are more than three or four years old.*

For small and medium-sized firms to offset this trend they need to exploit David versus Goliath advantages from the classic features of smaller scale.

Potentially, these include:

1. Greater speed of adaptation to changing market conditions through a less hierarchical management structure;
2. More rapid introduction of new technology and multi-skilled, multi-tasked labour;
3. Exploitation of reduced technical barriers of entry to new markets made possible in principle through flexible production.

Networking Regions

By the mid-1990s there was a rapid development of interregional cooperation policies sponsored by the European Commission. They had the virtue
of combining a strong local base with horizontal spatial integration.

In general these policies were agreements between regional
authorities spread over many fields including employment and social policy, education and training, culture, tourism, sports, infrastructure development etc).

There were two major types of such agreements:

1. *Cross-regional European Area* agreements: agreements between a
   greater number of regions that are geographically adjoined and therefore constituting bigger cross-national European areas (e.g. the Atlantic Arch cooperation, COTRAO, the proposal of the BALTIC Cooperation);

2. *Cross-regional Motors of Development* agreements: agreements between a limited number of regions that are not necessarily adjoined in
   geographical terms by *regions which, for various reasons, consider
   themselves as having common interests and common future prospects
   in Europe* (e.g. the *Four Motors for Europe,* the *Ouverture* project
   (cooperation between four Community regions (UK, D, E and I) with
   a view to cooperation with regions in Central and Eastern Europe.

   > *However, a major consequence of such interregional cooperation
   > is that the Centre and South-Centre of the Community is net-
   > worked, but the extreme South is still mainly excluded from such
   > networking. The same is also true for some of the northern regions
   > of the UK, and Northern Ireland.*

Networking Firms

While there is no doubt that the emergence of Interregional Networks is
immensely positive, and a major new dimension to a Europe of the Regions, it is, nonetheless, to be qualified on a range of grounds:

1. *Only one such initiative — the Four Motors agreement between Rhône-
   Alpes, Lombardy, Baden Wurtemberg and Catalonia — concerns regions which are not all geographically adjacent and focuses exclusively
   on networking firms;*

2. *Even the Four Motors initiative is, at present, restricted to R&D rather than other forms of cooperation between firms;*
3. *There is an understandable tendency in the new agreements between adjacent regions to focus on measures which can rationalize joint infrastructure, such as roads and communications;*
4. *Hard infrastructure cooperation may be desirable, but is not a sufficient condition for more effective joint cooperation by firms.*

  Such horizontal spatial integration needs to be reinforced by horizontal functional integration between-medium sized firms in the same or related sectors.

  It is through such interregional cooperation that some of the successful smaller firms, which otherwise will face barriers to their expansion in the new internal market, can gain some of the strengths of multinational companies without themselves becoming large multinationals.

As argued in a paper of July 1989 requested by Commissioner Gregory Varfis, after presentation of the case for networking at an earlier Athens conference by the author[3], the main form which can be achieved through this new interregional cooperation is for medium sized firms to promote flexible and specific agreements of the kind which can promote effective cooperation and minimise hierarchical conflict.

Such networking implies:

(1)   Flexible cooperation on:

1. *Basic and applied research*
2. *Design and product development*
3. *Joint component manufacture*
4. *Common computer software development*
5. *Joint advertising, including joint brand-naming;*
6. *Joint sales and export representation*

Such networking by firms also implies:

(2)   Flexible organization, with:

1. *Strategic alliances falling short of more inclusive agreements, such as mergers or joint ventures, and thus allowing a saving in transactions costs;*

2. *Specific agreements of the kind outlined in the context of flexible integration above;*
3. *An initial focus on agreements in those areas which are of most relevance to strengthening the joint competitive basis of such firms in the 1992 context;*
4. *Joint ventures or possibly mergers in the event of success with strategic alliances and specific agreements.*

By the mid-1990s the European Community had adopted a range of programmes which are compatible with the strategy on networking firms rather than simply networking adjacent regions. As illustrated below, these included RECITE, OUVERTURE, STRIDE, PRISMA, TELEMATIQUE and INTERREG.

However, while the RECITE [Regions and Cities of Europe] programme, launched in July 1991, was directly inspired by the concept of networking firms as argued above, it only provided for inter-firm networking indirectly under the general heading of cooperation between regional or local governments in promoting employment. Its main terms of reference covered a wide range of networking between regional or local authorities in other areas.

INTERREG networked only adjacent regions, and mainly in hard infrastructure projects, rather than the innovative entrepreneurial cooperation argued for in the 1989 paper prepared for Commissioner Varfis or the 1992 report on Economic and Social Cohesion for the 1990s made for Commission President Delors and other Commissioners.

The first phase of OUVERTURE was concerned with establishing virtually any kind of economic cooperation between the European Community and the newly independent countries of Central and Eastern Europe, and was based especially on the exchange of experience programmes. Within the framework of STRIDE, PRISMA and TELEMATIQUE, however, it was harder to find effective networks between smaller firms than between established mutlinational companies. The same was the case with the Third Framework Programme on Science and Technology.

An assessment of the limits on these grounds of the first round of interregional networking was submitted to President Delors and his Forward Planning Unit in 1993, during the preparation of the Delors White Paper on Growth Competitiveness and Employment.[4] Arguing that this first round has constituted mainly an exchange of experience without establishing links between firms, it submitted that the potential for networking by small and especially medium-sized firms in such programmes needed to be moved from the passive to an active mode.[5]

Reinforcing the arguments in the earlier report on economic and social cohesion of 1992[6], the paper submitted that the Commission should seek to synergize networking by measures which could:

1. Best develop European practice and the wide industrial and innovation role of MITI in Japan and other developmental States;
2. Identify the innovation frontiers in modern and entirely new sectors;
3. Assist small and medium-sized firms to approach and advance such innovation frontiers, rather than leave the lion's share of R&D programmes to big business.

In practice, this should involve:

1. Administrative guidance in those areas in which it will support R&D networking by SMEs in different Community regions;
2. Establishment and support for compatible and Community-wide innovation data banks of the kind recommended in the context of regional and local Innovation Centres;
3. Assistance for Community-wide networking - both of such Innovation Centres, and also of Regional Enterprise Agencies and Business Schools;
4. The creation of a Community public contracts information agency serving SMEs either directly or through the above type of institutions;
5. Sponsorship of joint advertising, sales and export representation by networked SMEs in both community and other international markets, thereby reinforcing scale effects in distribution of a kind which individual regional development agencies or local SMEs otherwise could not afford;
6. Reinforcement in this context of the OUVERTURE programme for networking with the reforming economies;
7. Establishment of a new programme to promote joint ventures between Regional Enterprise Agencies of Innovation Centres and the developing countries;
8. Centre-with-periphery networking to reinforce innovation, joint soft infrastructure and entrepreneurship programmes rather than centre-to-periphery financial transfers subsidising costs or resulting in mainly hard infrastructure.

Recent change

Most of the recent generation of Commission regional policies since 1995 reflect these new inperatives. Thus all projects under the new Article 10 of the European Regional Development Fund now must involve networks with at least one third of the partners coming from Objective 1 regions. Most of the programmes make provision for projects which involve both local development agencies and enterprises, with preference given to those which also involve local or regional RTD or Innovation Centres.

The new Objective IV of the Structural Funds provides financial assistance for the adaptation of enterprises to adapt to new methods of work organization; that is, in practice, the adoption of Japanese-style flexible or lean production. The new ADAPT programme is the international networking version of the new Objective IV.

Further, in the drafting of the Fourth Framework Programme on Science and Technology 1994-99 — in practice, the Industrial and Innovation Policy of the Union — real efforts were made to create conditions which could avoid the outcome of the first ESPRIT programme in which more than 70% of 5 billion ECU went to the research departments of only 12 giant firms. Thus, the Fourth Framework Programme provides preferential terms of access to its funding for small and medium-sized firms — essentially with no or few deadlines in project proposals — provided that they are themselves networked with at least two other firms in other regions of the Union.

Towards a Venture Capital Market for Small and Medium-sized firms

One of the main problems for innovative entrepreneurship — and networking — by small and medium-sized firms is the lack of a European venture capital market.

If firms are to network effectively in Europe they need finance for credit lines and equity for joint ventures. The same obtains for undertaking new joint ventures and reinforcing new export market potential in the intermediate reforming, industrialising and developing countries, notably those of Asia.

Much of this is lacking at present in many Member States of the Union where banks and other financial intermediaries take a highly conservative attitude to venture finance, insisting that entrepreneurs mortgage their properties, if not their companies, in return for credit at often penal rates of interest. In some Member States export credit guarantees are effective and efficient. In others they are cumbersome, bureaucratic, delayed and, understandably, spurned by firms themselves.

This is where the European Investment Fund (EIF) can and should play a key role. It was anticipated in its statutes in 1994 that it could by a decision of the board in June 1996 make equity investments in small and medium-sized firms.

So far the Fund has granted only loan guarantees on finance recycled from the European Investment Bank. Its board is composed of governments of the Member States, the EIB and the national and regional banks and credit institutions which subscribed its initial capital. This has been limited so far, and its loan guarantees restricted to less than 5 billion ECU. But its statutes foresaw that its capital could be increased to 7.5 billion ECU and its gearing ratio to 8, which would give a fund of 60 billion ECU.

If a third of this sum were allocated to a European venture capital market and the rest to regional finance on cohesion criteria, it could begin a transformation of the constrained prospects for the regions in the second half of the 1990s. Nor need the borrowings of the Fund be limited to this ceiling. There is a 360 billion ECU, or 6 per cent, excess of savings over investment in the GDP share of European OECD which needs to be recycled through public financial intermediation in actual investment projects.

This implies a crucial role for the regional financial intermediaries which are closest to the small and medium-sized firms needing the venture capital finance; and, inasmuch as these would be public financial intermediaries, the EIF could offer a clear net gain for European SMEs over their US counterparts; at least to the extent that US private venture capitalists have regularly insisted on the takeover of small and medium innovators by themselves and larger joint-venture distributors as the condition for receiving additional financing without penal interest rates during growth-expansion and international exports or joint ventures.

Offsetting Cohesion and through Union Credit and Equity Instruments

There have been two dire consequences of the efforts of governments to meet the 3 per cent GDP deficit and 60 per cent GDP debt conditions in the Treaty of Maastricht for the achievement of a single currency. The first has been a reduction in many national and regional programmes, such as the declaration in 1995 by the then Minister for the Mezzogiorno, Luigi Spaventa, that 'special programmes' for the South of Italy were peremptorily ended. The second was the degree to which national governments were unwilling to increase the Commission's 'own resources' through increased contributions from national taxation.

Under these constraints, compounded by the prospect that the major share of the claims on Structural Funds will be allocated to new Member States from Central and Eastern Europe within the next few years, it is hardly surprising that the Regional Commissioner, Wulf-Mathies, has been obliged to indicate to the various candidate-regions that the future of further financing — at least on the previous scale — is now in question.

It was in anticipation of such constrained public finances by national governments or from the Commission's own resources that the original proposal of the European Investment Fund was conceived and advanced in the 1992 report to President Delors.[7]

The essence of the case for the Fund — and its issue of Union Bonds as endorsed in the Delors White Paper[8] — was that, as a Union financial instrument, its borrowing would not be added to the Member States national debt provided that the loans were taken up by companies or regional governments or financial intermediaries rather than central governments.

A simple analogy can be made with US federal debt and expenditures financed through US Treasury bonds. This debt, and the cost of servicing such bonds, does not count on the debt of individual Member States of the federation such as California or Delaware.

Note: SME share allocated on basis of cohesion criteria. TEN share takes account of geographical position in terms of Objective 1 and Objective 2 criteria. 'Other' allocated on basis of population.

So far, the European Investment Fund has not allocated its funds on a regional basis. But the implications of at least a share of its lending and equity investments being undertaken on cohesion criteria of regional DGP and employment give results with both economic and political significance.

On this basis, as shown in Table 5.3 and estimated for a Union of 12 Member States, Germany would gain the higher absolute share (for the new 'Laender'), but the highest rates of increase of investment would be in Spain, Ireland, Portugal and Greece.

Table 5.3 Allocating a Share of 100 billion ECU EIF on Cohesion Criteria

	SME	Type of Project TEN (billion ECU)	Other	Total	Increase as percent of existing rate of investment
Denmark	0.2	0.1	0.1	0.4	2.5
France	2.3	1.7	1.3	5.4	2.6
Italy	2.8	1.1	1.3	5.2	2.7
Germany	4.4	3.4	1.8	9.6	3.2
Netherlands	0.8	0.6	0.4	1.7	3.2
UK	2.9	1.1	1.3	5.4	3.7
Belgium	0.5	0.5	0.2	1.3	3.8
Spain	3.3	2.5	0.9	6.6	5.4
Ireland	0.4	0.1	0.1	0.6	7.6
Portugal	1.2	0.4	0.2	1.8	7.8
Greece	1.3	0.5	0.2	2.0	12.4
Total	**20.0**	**12.0**	**8.0**	**40.0**	**3.6**

Evaluation, Scrutiny and Democratization

In 1996, a Europe of the Regions is for the making or breaking. The making is in process through the new dimensions by which old-style financial resource transfer from centre to periphery is giving way to new-style inter-regional cooperation between centre and periphery. Networking is not only a dimension of European regional policy. It has become the main thrust of such policy, as also employment and training through the ADAPT dimension to the new Objective IV and the networking conditions of the Fourth Framework Programme on Science and Technology.

However, European regional policy, even in this transformed mode, is now at a critical stage granted the relative limits on its own resources. It also needs to be effectively financed through an expansion of the borrowing and loan and equity investment potential of the European Investment Fund. This needs to be regionalised in a manner which can reinforce local credit and equity finance in not only small and medium-sized firms but also other areas of public and private financial partnerships.

Notably, the original terms of reference for the EIF included not only finance for small and medium-sized firms and the major transport and telecommunication networks of the TENs, but also environmentally safe energy projects. At the Brussels European Council the call was also made for the EIF to extend its financing to projects for urban regeneration.

So far, it has been only in January 1996 that the call has been made by the Commission President, Jacques Santer, and the then President of the European Council, Mr. Dini, for the EIF to actually issue Union Bonds to help finance the fourteen priority TENs projects selected by the Essen European Council, which, in turn, are a fraction of the 150 billion ECU to 550 billion ECU investment projects selected in the December 1993 Delors White Paper.

There also is the question of effective monitoring of the regional implications of the various current Commission programmes which have major regional implications. This includes not only the current phase of the implementation of the Structural Funds, and of the regional and cohesion implications of the TENs, but also the degree to which the Fourth Framework Programme for Science and Technology is in fact ensuring an advance in the share of funding for small and medium-sized firms rather than larger multinational enterprises.

Besides this, it is important that current policies for networking in the Fourth Framework Programme should be monitored to ensure that they promote rather than disseminate cohesion, and also for attention to the degree to which they, the ADAPT programme and applications for Innovative Measures within the European Regional Development Fund within its Article 10 programmes, both support networking between small and medium-sized firms and further reinforce the potential for the extension of joint trajectories of innovation by networked firms.

Some of this already is — and much of the rest should be — on the Agenda of the New Committee of the Regions and Local Government within the Commission's 1995 proposal for a new framework for surveillance of the implementation of Article 103 of the Treaty of Maastricht on the achievement of general economic policy objectives for the economies of the Member States of the Union.[9] In such a way the Committee of the Regions, with the European Parliament and the Social Partners, would have a real chance both to democratize the debate and to influence their own destiny.

Notes

1   Francois Perroux, La Notion de Pôle de Croissance, Economie Appliquée, 1955. Perroux later dismissed the concept of external economies as too opaque, and advocated more attention to the growth inducing effects of innovation [Les Techniques Quantitatives de la Planification, PUF, 1965].

2   Cecchini, P., The European Challenge 1992: The Benefits of a Single Market, Wildwood House, 1988.

3   Stuart Holland, The Promotion of Networking by Regional Development Agencies and Small and Medium Enterprise within the European Community, A Consultancy Paper for Commissioner Gregory Varfis, DG XVI, European Commission.

4   European Commission, White Paper on Growth, Competitiveness and Employment, Brussels, December 1993.

5   Stuart Holland, Cherchez la Firme! Paper submitted to the Forward Planning Unit of the President of the European Commission, 1993.

6   Stuart Holland, The European Imperative, op cit.

7   Stuart Holland, The European Imperative, ibid.

8   European Commission, White Paper on Growth and Competitiveness and Employment, op cit, part B.

9   See further attached figures and Stuart Holland, The European Imperative, op cit, chapter 1.2 (The Democratic Imperative).

Discussion by: Michael Steiner

Introduction

The need for new dimensions to regional theory and policy - not only in the European Union - is in theory undisputed albeit in practice, when policy-making, progressing only slowly. The scope and limits of traditional regional policies are, nowadays, broadly known and accepted, yet it seems difficult to implement - on all levels of policy-making for regions (regional, national, supranational) - these new insights into actual policies. Stuart Holland's paper can be regarded as a useful guide for overcoming the difficulties of implementation.

There seem to be two basic reasons for these difficulties of implementation (and Stuart Holland gives ample evidence of them):

1. The first is to be found in the practical problems of policy-making:
2. In the short-term character of policy-making, which runs counter to the often long-term character of the effects of new strategies and instruments; in the donor attitude which is connected with traditional instruments - giving and receiving cash for hardware investments is more popular for both sides than immaterial aid and soft infrastructure without a precise recipient; cooperative attitudes, relevant for new instruments to become effective, are not (yet) prevalent in many regions; delegation of power is difficult for both levels of decision-making - both for the level that has to give power and for the level gaining more influence; the latter often has neither the knowledge nor the attitude necessary for more responsibility.
3. The second reason lies in the still vague character of the new dimensions, especially its lack of analytical rigour and of causal links which pose problems of measurement, monitoring and evaluation. We know (or believe we know) which models work and which do not ('traditional analysis'); we are not yet sure about the working of the new model(s). The popularity of new dimensions conceals somewhat the lack of preciseness. New catchwords abound such as 'cooperation', 'cluster orientation', 'networking', 'synergy creation'. Being aware of the dangers of the popularity of old and new catchwords, one should keep in mind Machlup's criticism of almost 40 years ago against the use of 'weasel words and jargon' in economics alluding to the extreme use of the word 'structure'. Substituting the word 'structure' by 'cooperation, cluster, etc.' you can use the expression without difficulty: 'The word structure'

(= cooperation, network, cluster etc.) works in some educated circles just as the phrase 'you know what I mean' works among less literate people. To persuade you that a certain measure is needed, you are told that the 'structure' (= network character) makes it absolutely indispensable, and that the 'structural imbalance' (= missing network) cannot be coped with in any other way, - surely, you understand, don't you?' Machlup (1958).

It is the merit of Stuart Holland's paper to point out both kinds of difficulties, i.e., those of theory and of policy, and to go beyond the weasel-word character of new insights and to give selective advice to diminish the implementation problem.

It is a condensed survey on recent developments and insights into regional and industrial economics, and as such it points to new factors of regional development, such as endogenous potential, to human factors - qualifications and entrepreneurship; immobility of these factors; to the importance of the local and regional milieus, of networking, of the importance of SMEs and their shortcomings.

It states the necessary policy consequences (as outlined in Table 5.1 and Table 5.2 of Stuart Holland's paper) thereby also differentiating between different levels of policy-making, and it touches on the question of regionalization in the sense of democratization. For this reason the question of subsidiarity is raised.

It stresses - directly and indirectly - open questions and the shortcomings both of theory and policy, and touches in a delicate way the question of financing regional policy on the European level.

In the spirit of this workshop - 'Desiderata for a Further Development of European Spatial Development Policies' - I would like to concentrate my discussion on one of the open questions emphasized by Stuart Holland and point to conceptual and empirical approaches (and difficulties) in defining networks (clusters, complexes, etc.). This approach is, in fact, an old topic in a new setting for regional and industrial analysis and policy. The concept of networks (industrial districts, growth poles, clusters, complexes, etc.) comes from the idea that interlinked activities which, frequently, are regionally concentrated create synergies, increase productivity and lead to economic advantages. Hence, policy should create, develop and support such networks.

Empirical attempts to show the existence of, and or to find, such networks date back to the 1940s. They were revived by growth pole concepts[10] and received a new impetus by the empirically based cluster concept by Porter. The famous 'diamond' links locational factors, demand aspects, firm-specific strategies with interconnected activities to get a hold on a region's/nation's competitiveness.

The conceptual and empirical difficulties stem from the question on what really constitutes a network: material linkages, immaterial networks, tacit forms of knowledge-exchange, infrastructural and infostructural preconditions? Depending on the theoretical perspectives and the subsequent answers, different methodological concepts and data needs for analysis will follow.

We will point to theoretical approaches concerning such (regional) networks, then give examples for an empirical foundation in a regional context for Austria (how to measure networks, what data are needed to define them) and finally give some conclusions for the analysis and interpretation of the network idea.

Theoretical approaches

Simple as it seems and old as it is, the idea of industrial networks/clusters represents quite a challenge not only for orthodox economic theorizing and for traditional economic policy, but also for usual statistical ways to define production systems and for the analysis of competitive advantages. This idea presumes that

1. The existence of clusters and complexes is the decisive element for competitiveness of regions and nations and not cheap land, labour, energy, high subsidies and low social costs, but also not high technology and strong leading industries;
2. There is a need for firms to develop new strategies: instead of an individual 'search for excellence' they have to go in for a cooperative 'as a group we are stronger' situation; this reflects partly the new practice of business behaviour, and it also reflects new insights into innovative and organisational approaches;
3. Feedback mechanisms replace linear causalities; the multidimensionality of factors influencing competitiveness - Porter's 'diamond' identifies four groups of factors (locational factors, demand, market structure and corresponding strategies of firms, clusters of interlinked and supporting industries) - escapes a monocausal relationship;
4. We have to look for new ways of defining productive systems that go beyond the usual concept of industries, and - in a wider sense - we have to find new methods and data to indicate (regional) technological change.

One of the first economists to point out the advantages of clustered economic activity was, of course, Marshall (1920), who argued that firms and industries do behave in a way which may question a static theory of perfect competition. Instead they exhibit properties and form industrial structures that today are known as network models, industrial districts, complexes and clusters. It is exactly because of these elements in his theory that Marshall is known - at least for economists interested in industrial relations and regional problems - for his way of thinking in the field of 'localization', and because he offers a very early and precise formulation for the advantages of localized industries. He emphasized three reasons for cluster formation: labour market effects, supply linkages and technological spill-overs.

A parallel line of thinking was developed by location and agglomeration theory. Classical location theory starts from the fact that there is an uneven distribution of economic activity in space; these activities are concentrated in relatively few centres, and in some regions these centres are stronger than in others. Neither regions nor centres have to have the same size nor similar structures. Classical location theorists start either from the supply side or from the demand side to explain concentrations of activity: Weber (1909) points besides transport costs and regional differences in wages to advantages connected with spatial closeness: regional concentration creates benefits for production; Lösch (1940) and, very similarly, Christaller (1933) regard the advantage of agglomeration as caused by a large market.

Hoover (1937) was the first to systematically categorize these advantages and to point out the different influences for spatial production costs:

1. Economies of scale within a firm resulting from size and/or an increase in the amount of production;
2. Localization economies arising for all firms in a single industry at a single location, subsequent to the enlargement of the total output of that industry at that location;
3. Urbanization economies accruing to all firms in all industries at a single location, consequent upon the enlargement of total size (population, income, output or wealth) of that location, for all industries taken together.

This three-fold division of agglomeration advantages is still largely undisputed, yet there are interpretative differences as to their economic character. Mostly they are regarded as economies of scale due to indivisibilities and specialization, and leading to a reduction in the stock of specialized inputs necessary for production by a single firm (with the convenient empirical side-effect of being measurable by means of a production function approach). Yet Hoover's original definition emphasizes their character of externalities: localization and urban economies are external advantages which prevail if the production (or cost) function of one firm is influenced by others, whereby other firms do not intend to exert such an influence and/or are not compensated for it. The essential point is the fact that firms have to accept these influences without being able to do anything about them themselves, i.e. they are not able to produce these effects.

A further distinction is important: agglomeration advantages arise more often out of 'economies of scope' rather than out of 'economies of scale' Goldstein (1984). This means that an essential reason for the concentration of economic activity consists of the incentive to reduce the costs of coordination of closely linked activities. Agglomerations may be regarded as an 'engine' for spatial integration in the same sense as vertically integrated firms gain efficiency advantages by means of multi-output production - it is not simply the scale effect of a region, but the improvement of productive efficiency through the means of a common location for interlinked activities. This idea comes very close to Marshall again and to arguments used by industrial economists for the integration of firms Scherer (1980) Williamson (1981): an enforced control of the economic environment, a safer delivery of inputs in situations of scarcity, protection of price pressure by monopolists, and higher market penetration.

Exactly these ideas - influenced by industrial economics and organisation theory - led to the revival of the consideration of synergy effects and networks, better known nowadays under the heading 'cluster-concept'.

The recent attractiveness of the cluster concept - in its best known version formulated by Porter (1990) - has three distinct (theoretical) roots:

1. The concept of scale economies has brought about a change of emphasis in recent economic theorizing (Tichy 1995), and the neo-classical inspired model of perfect competition has been replaced by models of oligopoly. The new growth theory (Romer 1987) and the theory of foreign trade (Helpmann 1985) emphasize scale effects which are external to the firm but internal to the economy. These effects might be due to learning effects which, through improved investment and mobility of the work-force, can be transferred to other firms, or they might result from specialized inter-industrial supply. Krugman (1991) points to the critical factors necessary for the rise (and further existence) of such

complexes: transport costs, agglomeration advantages, fixed costs (leading to scale effects). In his models there is also room for real effects of expected and hoped-for advantages in specific locations: centres might rise and grow because people believe they have better chances there - self-fulfilling prophecies arising out of the belief in agglomeration advantages.

2. A second line of arguments stems from new literature on the theory of the firm and from the actual behaviour of firms. The new literature points to bounded rationality (Simon 1983), to a change from mass-production to flexible automatization (Piore 1984), to the path-dependency of search processes of innovative firms (Nelson 1982), to organisational preconditions for successful innovation both within and outside the firms (Constant 1984, Auerbach 1988, Chandler 1990). These new insights into behavioural aspects of firms pointing to limited knowledge, uncertainties and organisational and social embeddedness are backed by the actual strategies of firms: The rush for diversification and conglomerates has been replaced by 'back to basics' and 'concentration on core activities' strategies. Instead of an individual firm-specific 'search for excellence', the need for cooperation and for strategic alliances has been emphasized and, more often than before, even exercised; instead of isolated firms, firm-clusters promise higher success.

3. The third factor lies in the new character of technological knowledge and technological change.

   - The traditional choice between entrepreneurism and large, hierachically-structured firms cannot be maintained anymore, because R&D costs are escalating well beyond the capabilities of firms, and the knowledge in a firm is marked by a high level of specificity impeding a firm's future learning capabilities and knowledge transfer;

   - This approach is increased by the fact that innovative skill and information are increasingly non-cumulative, heterogeneous and strain internal capabilities;

   - The diversification of demand aggravates the problem by necessitating frequent production reorganisation, imposing difficult considerations between commitment to existing investments, on the one hand, and flexibility of response, on the other;

   - Shorter product life-cycles force firms to enter all markets simultaneously, yet few firms independently control this kind of global

distribution capacity or possess a range of such specialized market knowledge;
- The historical boundaries between industries alter or dissolve, the same is true between high technology and traditional sectors;
- Technological change does not necessarily favour small or large firms, nor does market differentiation automatically eliminate economies of scale in finance, design or marketing.

These developments have as a consequence that the spatial distance to research, development and transfer institutions, but also to clients, cooperation partners, service firms and (semi)public institutions, becomes a central determinant of innovative activities. The regional dimension, i.e. the specific constellation of these factors within regions, gains importance. Regional networks therefore have manifold dimensions.

Some empirical examples in the context of Austrian regions

The idea of regional networks evidently has many roots and diverse theoretical foundations. Not surprisingly there are different empirical approaches to identify such networks. In order to exemplify such approaches a few empirical studies in the context of Austria's regional setting will be reported.

Input-output linkages and spatial association One of the first methodological approaches to measure agglomerative tendencies and to verify the existence of spatial complexes compared material linkages between sectors and the spatial concentration of these sectors: do input-output linkages lead to spatial concentration? Starting with Florence (1944) and continued by Streit (1969), Richter (1969), Czamanski/Czamanski (1977) and Harrigan (1982), this approach starts with the assumption that 'industrial agglomerations are not due or not only due to the common attraction to urban centres but to interaction among the various industries' (Czamanski/Czamanski 1977). Industrial complexes accordingly are defined by the linkage of industries by input and output flows and their locational vicinity.

Using an input-output table and sector employment data at the district level (the lowest regional level with a consistant database) Kubin/Steiner (1987) showed for Austria different degrees of intensity of regional industrial (and also service-oriented) complexes. By means of correlation coefficients, cluster analysis and graph-theoretical methods, different intensities of 'functional' linkages (i.e. input-output linkages) and 'spatial association' (i.e. an equal distribution of sector employment across all regional units) were compared.

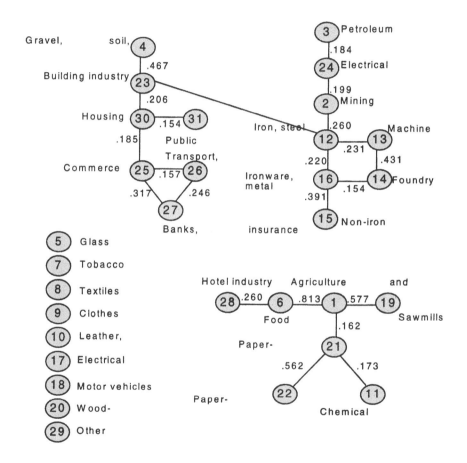

Figure 5.1 Graph of Functional Linkages

Source: Kubin/Steiner (1987)

Figure 5.1 shows the graph of functional linkages of 31 sectors with different intensities of input-output relations.

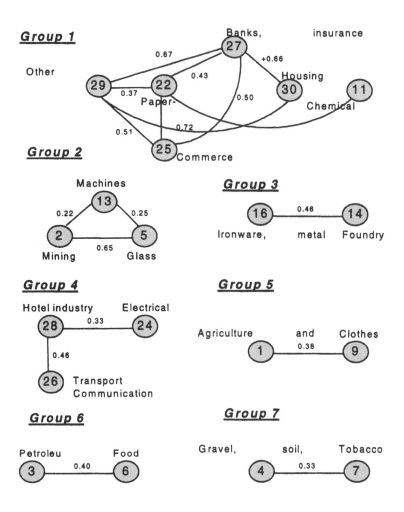

Figure 5.2 Groups of Industries with Spatial Association

Source: Kubin/Steiner (1987)

Figure 5.2 shows groups of sectors being spatially associated (the numbers represent correlation coefficients indicating the degree of equal distribution of sector employment).

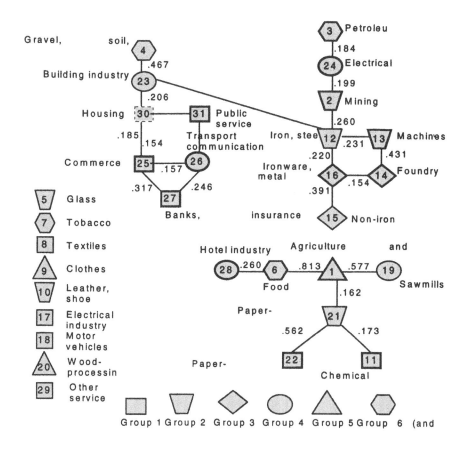

Figure 5.3 Graph with Combination of Functional Linkage and Spatial Association

Source: Kubin/Steiner (1987)

Figure 5.3 indicates the 'coincidence' of functional linkages between sectors and their spatial concentration (the graphical symbols such as circles, triangles etc. stand for the spatial concentration of the respective sectors, the functional relations being as in Figure 12): only a small part of all sectors has linkages that lead to spatial concentration. This refutes somewhat the classical hypothesis of location theory - (which is that) regional industrial complexes are to a small extent caused by material linkages.[11]

Competitive clusters In search of other dimensions of regional clusters the Porter approach was used with some modifications. The basis for its regional application was a study by t.i.p. (an Austrian institution for technology - information - policy consultancy; Peneder 1994) where the competitiveness of Austria's industry was analysed by means of diverse internal and external factors such as international market shares, foreign trade specialization, the degree of international division of labour, export distances and also measures of productivity and profitability. The aim of this study was to link sectors and product groups to different levels of competitiveness.[12]

Using this basic information on the whole of Austria's industry a group of researchers at InTeReg (Steiner 1996) tried to transfer these data to the industrial structure of Styria (one of the nine provinces of Austria) to find out to what extent competitive clusters are present in this region. The result is shown in Figure 5.4. In this matrix, clusters with different degrees of competitiveness (as identified for the whole of Austria) are aligned with different intensities of representation for these industries in Styria. A high degree of competitiveness with, simultaneously, a strong representation in Styria can be found in the production of steam-boilers, leather, iron and rails. In general, the results show that Styria has a considerable portion of Austria's highly competitive sectors and can be interpreted as a regional concentration and clustering of industries. Yet these sectors represent only a small part of the whole of Styria's industry, and are to be regarded rather as innovative niches of successful firms within the total of rather traditional industries.

Technological clusters Technological clusters are based on the idea that firms having a similar patent structure are also technologically similar and therefore form such 'technological clusters'. Firms within such clusters are able - according to this thesis - to use technological overspills. In contrast, firms which concentrate their production on single technologies - within their environment - have little chance of benefiting from external effects.

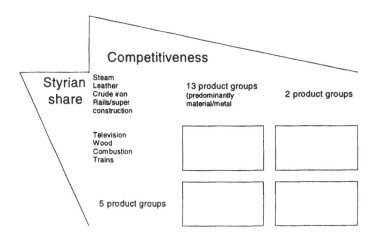

Figure 5.4 Cluster

Source: Peneder (1996), Steiner et al. (1996)

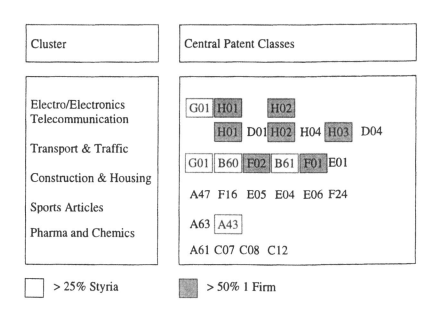

Figure 5.5 Technological Cluster

Source: Hutschenreiter (1994), Steiner et al. (1996)

Such technological clusters were - based on Jaffe (1989) - extracted for Austria Kuklinski (1994). Firms with similar patent activities were structured and grouped into clusters. By these means it is possible to identify potential 'horizontal spill-overs' between firms with similar technological activities: informal contacts, exchange of information, a common pool of qualified workers and a common educational and research infrastructure are examples of such horizontal linkages.

For Austria as a whole there were five large fields with firms having a similar patent structure: electro/electronics, transport, construction, sport articles, pharmaceuticals/chemicals. When using the same approach as for competitive clusters to regionalize this data-set, the results for Styria showed the following pattern Steiner (1996):

In Figure 5.5 those patent classes are marked which have a strong representation in (more than 25%) of Styrian firms; whereas in the two clusters of construction and pharmaceuticals/chemicals Styria is only weakly represented, the clusters electro/electronics and transport are dominated by Styrian firms. This again can be interpreted in favour of the existence of regional clusters or complexes: technologically similar firms are regionally concentrated.

Yet these basically positive results (from a Styrian perspective) have to be qualified: rather small technological niches within these fields play a dominant role; it is mostly small and medium-sized firms which concentrate on a specific field of technology within the patent class and, more important, the number of firms is rather small, i.e. many patents are performed by a limited group of innovative firms so that the potential for spill-overs is reduced.

Cooperative behaviour and immaterial networks To complement this regional cluster-oriented analysis of competitiveness, technological cooperation and linkages, a survey of Styrian firms (with more than 20 employees) was conducted to find out about their strategies toward the year 2000, their market situation and their competitive pressure Steiner (1996). A special emphasis was put on the strategic and cooperative behaviour to obtain information on the tendency and the willingness to form immaterial networks. Concentrating on the relative importance of cooperation as an entrepreneurial strategy for the future, the firms were asked what their strategic priorities for the next decade were.

The strategies pursued can be largely divided into three groups: very important strategies (more than 80% of the responding firms consider them as decisive), important ones (more than 40% of the firms regarded them as decisive), less important ones (less than 40%). The following, for example, were regarded as very important strategies: orientation towards higher qualification, quality, looking for market niches; orientation towards clients and the opening markets in Eastern Europe. Altogether, Styrian firms pursue an offensive, market-oriented strategy. Yet, cooperative strategies are considered to be of minor importance. Only 27% of the firms intend to cooperate with other firms, 34% with research institutions, and 26% with production-oriented services. The strongest form of cooperation is considered to be informal contacts (41% of the responding firms). This points to a low readiness for networking and (strategic) alliances. In combination with the other information concerning cooperation (as presented above) where a low degree of cooperation can be obtained, this additional piece of information reveals that firms obviously have little interest and intention to do so in the future. Forming complexes by means of (formal and informal) cooperation and alliances is not a decisive strategy.

Conclusions

What do these theoretical considerations and illustrative empirical approaches to regional networks (clusters, complexes, growth poles, etc.) tell us?

This is hard to say exactly. Which approach is the correct one is still an open question. The concept arose out of the criticism of the existing statistical nomenclature and its inability to define the 'correct' units of economic activity. The beginning is marked by attempts to find a better description of the production system than those of industries and its subdivisions.

For this reason input-output flows seemed appropriate. They mirror material linkages beween the statistically separate industries. Yet our empirical example - well in line with other studies - suggests that these material linkages lead, apart from a few cases, to spatial vicinity; and then do so for only a few 'old' weight and transport intensive industries. From the theoretical point of view input-output flows have a 'vertical' bias and miss important immaterial ('horizontal') connections. Additionally, from an empirical point of view, this approach has the disadvantage that for an analysis on a lower regional basis the necessary input-output tables do not exist in most cases.

Material linkages alone do not yet constitute a cluster. A cluster pre-supposes a network of innovative partners. Such a network is not based on outsourcing and subcontracting but on a common knowledge: a cluster is a network-like system of information and not a system of material supply.

These immaterial and horizontal aspects are more strongly represented in technological clusters. Our empirical analysis points towards regional concentrations of such clusters. Yet a still closer look raises some doubts whether these horizontal external effects really exist on a lower regional basis. The number of patents and its concentration in patent classes is rather high, while the number of patenting firms is rather low.

These technological clusters together with the competitive clusters nevertheless stress the regional dimension of clusters. The cited examples for Styria support the spatial aspect of complexes. Starting off from a national analysis, Styria is in some national clusters rather weakly represented, but dominates in others - there are distinct and strong regional concentrations of closely associated activities.

This regional dimension is supported also by the importance of tacit knowledge and informal communication. This aspect refutes to a certain degree the arguments for a declining importance of cluster concepts and its antispatial dimensions: progress in telecommunications and internet communication structures may render face-to-face contacts superfluous and may link long distant partners immediately. The question is still open and disputable but - as many case studies show - most new ideas and projects have arisen out of intensive personal cooperation and informal contacts. These do demand spatial proximity (otherwise we would not need conferences and workshops).

Regional complexes are not only industrial. Services - especially producer-oriented, but not only these - are an essential part of clusters and include research institutions, marketing organisations, specialized financial and juridical services. Finally, also cultural elements influencing the 'milieu innovateur' play an important role.

There is no 'correct' concept of networks and clusters. It depends on the aim of analysis and is therefore 'teleological'. That is no relief, quite the contrary, as it forces both the theorist, the empirical researcher and the policy-maker to define what he wants to know and how to find it out by means of empirically based analysis.

Notes

10   For a survey of both conceptual-theoreticl approaches and of empirical case studies of the growth pole idea see Kuklinski [31].

11   For a more comprehensive presentation of the methodological approach and the results see Kubin / Steiner (1987).

12   A slightly different approach to obtain competitive clusters was used by Clemet (1995).

References

Auerbach, P. (1988), Competition. The Economics of Industrial Change, Basil Blackwell, Oxford.

Chandler, A. D. (1990), Scale and Scope: The Dynamics of Industrial Capitalism, Harvard U.P., Belknap Press, Cambridge/London.

Christaller, W. (1933), Die zentralen Orte in Süddeutschland, Fischer, Jena.

Clement, W. (1995), Cluster und ihre industriepolitischen Konsequenzen in Österreich, in: Steiner, M., (ed., 1995) Regionale Innovation. Durch Technologiepolitik zu neuen Strukturen, Leykam, Graz.

Constant, E. W. (1984), Communities and Hirarchies: Structure in the Practice of Science and Technology, in: R. Laudan (ed.), *The Nature of Technological Knowledge*, Reidel, Dordrecht, Boston.

Czamanski, D., Czamanski, St. (1977), Industrial Complexes: Their Typology, Structure and Relation to Economic Development, *Papers of the Regiona Science Association*, Vol. 38, 93 - 111.

Florence, S. (1944), The Selection of Industries Suitable for Dispersion into Rural Areas, *Journal of the Royal Statistical Society*, Vol. 107, 93 - 116.

Goldstein, G./Gronberg, T. (1984), Economics of Scope and Economics of Agglomeration, *Journal of Urban Economics*, Vol. 16, 91 - 104.

Harrigan, F. (1982), The Relationship between Industrial and Geographical Linkages: A Case Study of the United Kingdom, *Journal of Regiona Science*, Vol. 22, 19 - 31.

Helpman, E., Krugman, P. (1985), Market Structure and Foreign Trade, MIT Press, Cambridge, Mass.

Hoover, E., (1937), Location Theory and the Shoe and Leather Industries, Harvard University Press, Cambridge.

Hutschenreiter, G. (1994), Cluster innovativer Aktivitäten in der österreichischen Industrie, Studie im Auftrag des Bundesministeriums f. öffentliche Wirtschaft und Verkehr sowie für Wissenschaft und Forschung, t.i.p., Wien.

Jaffc, A.B. (1989), 'Characterizing the 'Technological Position' of Firms, with Application to Quantifying Technological Opportunity and Research Spillovers', *Research Policy*, Vol. 18, 87 - 97.

Krugman, P. (1991), Geography and Trade, Leuven U.P., MIT Press, Leu.

Kubin, I., Steiner, M. (1987), Muster räumlicher und funktionaler Verbindung, mimeo, Dpt. of Economics, University of Graz.

Kubin, I., Steiner, M. (1987), Muster räumlicher und funktionaler Verbindung, mimeo, Dpt. of Economics, University of Graz.

Kuklinski, A. (ed. 1972), Growth Poles and Growth Centres in Regional Planning, Mouton, Paris.

Lösch, A. (1940), Die räumliche Ordnung der Wirtschaft, Fischer, Jena.

Machlup, F. (1958), Structure and Structural Change: Weaselwords and Jargon. Zeitschrift für Nationalökonomie, 18, 233 - 260.

Marshall, A. (1920), Principles of Economics, Macmillan, London.

Nelson, R., Winter, S. (1982), An Evolutionary Theory of Economic Change, Harvard University Press, Cambridge.

Peneder, M. (1994), Clusteranalyse und sektorale Wettbewerbsfähigkeit der österreichischen Industrie, Studie im Auftrag des Bundesministeriums f. öffentliche Wirtschaft und Verkehr sowie für Wissenschaft und Forschung, t.i.p., Wien.

Piore, M., Sabel, Ch. (1984), The Second Industrial Divide. Possibilities for Prosperity. Basic Books, New York.

Porter, M. (1990), The Competitive Advantage of Nations, Free Press, New York.

Richter, Ch. (1969), The Impact of Industrial Linkages on Geographic Association, *Journal of Regiona Science*, Vol. 9, 19 - 27.

Romer, T. M. (1987), Growth Based on Increasing Returns due to Specialisation of the European Communities, in: *American Economic Review*, Vol. 77 (2), 56 - 62.

Scherer, F. (1980), Industrial Market Structure and Economic Performance, McNally, Chicago.

Simon, H. (1983), Reason in Human Affairs, Basil Blackwell, Oxford.

Steiner, M., Jud, Th., Pöschl, A., Sturn, D. (1996), Ein Technologiepolitisches Konzept für die Steiermark, Leykam, Graz (forthcoming).

Streit, M. (1969), Spatial Associations and Economic Linkages between Industries, *Journal of Regional Science*, Vol. 9, 177 - 188.

Tichy, G. (1995), Die wirtschaftspolitische Bedeutung ökonomisch-technischer Cluster Konzepte, in: Steiner, M., (ed., 1995) Regionale Innovation. Durch Technologiepolitik zu neuen Strukturen, Leykam, Graz.

Weber, A., (1909), Über den Standort der Industrien, Mohr/Siebeck, Tübingen.

Williamson, O. (1981), The Modern Corporation: Origins, Evaluation, Attributes, *Journal of Economic Literature*, Vol.19, 1537 - 1568.

6 A Plea for Cooperative Strategies for Europe

EGON MATZNER

Socio-economic processes as positive, zero and negative sum games

Socio-economic processes are usually interpreted and evaluated according to their inputs and the outcomes achieved. Let us take two examples: a) the money supply policy of the central bank, and the changes in the price level; and b) the allocation of financial resources to regions, and the changes in productivity and employment levels. The conventional mode which connects inputs and outputs of socio-economic processes is the means-ends model as formalized by the late Jan Tinbergen (1956). The Tinbergen model of economic and social policy has its merits but also some significant shortcomings (Matzner 1994). One of the major deficiencies is its simplistic input structure: it does not make strategic behaviour explicit. A second weakness relates to the links between (political) input and (socio-economic) outcome: it neither clarifies the agents' situation in which they decide and act, nor does it reflect the dichotomy between intended and unintended outcomes. A third reason for looking for a supplementary approach can be found in the blindness of the model with regard to genuine uncertainty.

Game theory offers such a supplementary approach. It also connects inputs and outputs. But the inputs are the strategic behaviour of political, economic, social, etc. agents. The outcome belongs to one of the following three types.

1. *A positive sum:* The agents involved succeed in achieving an increase of e.g. value added and/or other values. Each 'player' can be remunerated by the 'increase of the cake'.
2. *A zero sum:* The agents involved do not achieve an increase. The increase of a player's remuneration is the loss of an other player.

3. *A negative sum:* The agents involved cannot prevent by their decision and action a decrease, e.g. in the value added, they may even contribute to it. Losses for players emerge and have to be distributed.

As to the 'input side' of the socio-economic processes, which produce the above mentioned outputs, two types of strategic behaviour can be discerned:

1. *Cooperative strategies:* They comprise a behaviour of two or more agents aimed at achieving in the aggregate, a positive sum. Cooperation for the purpose of this analysis comprises non-cooperative games that result in positive sums. In a dynamic setting, cooperative games with a positive sum outcome are self-enforcing to a *virtuous circle*. *Examples* of cooperative behaviour are unions' wage bargaining, which avoids cost-push inflation; or obeying traffic rules, which reduces traffic casualties.
2. *Non-cooperative strategies:* These comprise a form of behaviour that does not care about the interests of the other player(s). If repeated, it results in a zero sum. It can end up in a *vicious circle* of negative sum games.

In the sphere of regional and spatial development, we know that positive sum games as results of cooperative behaviour, as well as zero sum and negative sum games, coexist. It corresponds to Myrdal's world of circular causation with cumulative effects (Myrdal 1956).

Where do market processes belong?

Which games are involved in the market processes? In the 'ideal' world of 'pure' markets, we encounter all types of results. According to consumer preferences, output will either grow, remain at a particular level or fall. Suppliers who compete in the market have to adapt to this reality. Their decisions and actions do not have an influence on anything else but on the product they offer on the market. Problems, such as inflation, depression, pollution, etc., are non-existent, unless they are elements of individual preferences. There is a fair division of outputs and inputs. Cooperative behaviour means obeying the rules of fair competition and free expression of the consumer's sovereignty. There is no problem of regional imbalance or social conflict. Strategic behaviour does not exist in the pure market model.

The 'pure' market model has, of course, only little resemblance to the real market processes (Morgenstern 1972). In the latter, the just mentioned problems occur because one actor's decision has a negative or positive effect on others: there are simply no production or distribution processes without recourse to (limited) resources or without unavoidable waste (Georgescu-Roegen 1971). There are interdependencies between suppliers as well as between consumers. Of course, there is strategic behaviour at stake. Positive, zero and negative sum games occur even if suppliers adapt to consumer preferences. One reason is, of course, that firms shape preferences. But as Schelling (1978) has shown, even in the absence of, for example, manipulative advertisement, utility maximization may give unintended results. Therefore, it is necessary to analyse real-type market processes in which cooperative behaviour is not just restricted to obeying the code of good competitive behaviour and of consumer sovereignty. Cooperation and non-cooperative behaviour have to be analysed in those areas where private and public interests diverge, as in the fields of inflation, mass unemployment, regional imbalances, pollution, etc.

It is important to understand that divergence between private and public interests was of crucial concern to the English classical political economists. Contrary to widespread beliefs in public debate as well in the scientific community, Adam Smith did not believe that 'the market' will harmoniously bring about an equalization of private and public costs and benefits of economic activities. On the contrary, English classical political economists did not even believe in the magic of the 'invisible hand'. For them, the 'invisible hand" was not the hand of competition in the market. To their understanding, it was the hand of the law-giver, '... the hand which withdraws from the sphere of the pursuit of self-interest those possibilities which do not harmonise with the public good'. They even conclude that '...the pursuit of self-interest, unrestrained by suitable institutions, carry no guarantee of anything except chaos. Moreover, these institutions are not natural in the sense that they arise inevitably' (Robbins 1978, p.56). In this sense, the spirit of the classical economists calls for an institutionally regulated competition in the market. This view contradicts the 'old', nowadays again very popular, ideology that says competition is the panacea irrespective of the divergence between private and public interests.

Where does the EU stand?

The process of Western European integration, both in programme and in reality, is geared towards the promotion of competitive market processes.

The Four Freedoms are ends in themselves and they are also the most important instruments in achieving Union-wide economic integration. Market fundamentalists, who are not that rare among politicians and economists, believe that social cohesion will emerge; and some even believe that the Four Freedoms will also induce a political Union in the end. In the process of European integration, there are also interventionist influences at work. The outcome of the two opposing tendencies are the rules of the 'European game'. They give evidence to the compromises achieved by the two parties. They can be observed as legislative (or better 'commissionary') norms as well as in the field of European institution-building. The European Court, and its norms for controlling and enacting competitive rules, clearly shows that, on balance, competition weighs much more than cooperation. This imbalance is even more evident if rules, standards, and the power of institutions in areas such as social security, environment, or regional and structural policies are brought into the picture. The single example of a dominance of intervention over competition is the large area of agricultural policy. One can, however, hardly say that, in this area, the established rules are particularly successful in bringing private and public interests closer.

The next area of regulation, actually in the process of being established, is the monetary system. Although the Maastricht Treaty gives clear dominance to the market fundamentalist view, the monetary terrain is still more or less heavily contested and will remain so. The way envisaged for introducing the single currency is guided by an overall objective, namely, to secure monetary stability. The way to it is paved with convergence criteria which clearly is an exercise comparable to tying down Ulysses when tempted by the Sirens (in this case, by higher deficit). Ultra-fundamentalists suggest further tightening of the convergence criteria. According to the Maastricht Treaty, no other objective is allowed to come close to the rank of public purpose. Cooperative behaviour, which we defined as behaviour being in accordance with a public purpose, is thus restricted to the monetary area. All other policy objectives, such as full employment, social security and regional balance, are subordinated to monetary stability.

The emerging dominance of non-cooperative behaviour and zero/negative sum games

If this perception of the integration of (Western) Europe is correct, we are participating in a process in which non-cooperative behaviour and the ensuing zero or negative sum outcomes are gaining influence. Perhaps they have already achieved dominance.

I should like to draw your attention to the area which is most influential for socio-economic and political relations. It is the world monetary order. I shall do that because money is also of crucial importance for spatial developments, although this is generally overlooked. (I shall take up the issue of money and space explicitly in section 6).

Why is the present international monetary system as determined by the International Monetary Fund and the World Bank an example of non-cooperative behaviour and a zero sum game? As we all know, the IMF's task is to safeguard international exchange as well as to provide it with sufficient international liquidity. The main concern of the IMF, therefore, relates to imbalances in the payment between nations. Payment imbalances caused by a deficit of one country and a surplus of other countries are — according to the rules of the IMF — to be settled unilaterally and only by the debtor country. It has to restrict its domestic demand to the point at which imports reach the level of exports. Thus, of course, the exports of another country will also be restricted. This is a negative sum game in the pure sense: the sum of output of creditor and debtor countries is thus reduced, both (or all) players lose by this rule coined by Keynesians as the 'asymmetric adaptation mechanism'. If we look beyond the field of monetary policy, cooperation by obeying the present rules of the IMF game amounts to non-cooperative behaviour in the real economy of commodities, services and employment, as it contributes to its reduced growth. There is no lack of ideas on how to design an international monetary system which does not necessitate non-cooperative behaviour on both debtor and surplus country sides (Tobin 1982). Their case is simple: it is the establishment of a 'symmetric adaptation mechanism' in which both the debtor and creditor countries share the responsibility for reducing the imbalances; the one by restricting the level of economic activity, and the other by stimulating it. By such a balancing mechanism the reduction of effective demand in the system could be avoided.

It should be clear that the consolidation policies imposed on all EU member countries amount to a EU-wide reduction of effective demand, hence output and employment. It is a large-scale exercise in asymmetric adaptation with no compensating mechanism. It has been called a competition in deflationist policies in the absence of inflation. The dominance of such a monetary objective imposes non-cooperative behaviour in the form of massive cuts in public expenditure in the presence of growing unemployment, urban and regional decay, and growing numbers of the poor and homeless.

The spatial dimension of (non-) cooperation

What is cooperative behaviour in the spatial dimension? In line with my statement we first have to agree about what would be the public purpose in the spatial dimension. The public purpose in the spatial dimension can be defined as behaviour that reduces productivity and income differentials between regions. Non-cooperative behaviour would accordingly comprise decisions and actions which neither reduce nor increase these differentials.

Regional imbalances result from the uneven distribution of productive forces, such as the supply of human resources (including entrepreneurial talents) and provision of financial means, either fostered or impeded by socio-economic institutions. The same applies to the social and cultural infrastructure as well as to the size of a region. The way poor and rich parts interrelate is, of course, not only to be determined by the regions in question. It is the overall system and its rules which are also crucial. It is clear that regional development would be stimulated, if the 'stock' of entrepreneurial personalities were increased. A 'fast breeder' of such talents is not yet available. We know quite well that regional development is also determined by the availability of financial resources. Simply channelling funds, however, is by no means sufficient to stimulate development. It is also important that the region has a minimum size of, say, 5 to 15 million inhabitants and a good infrastructure (from international schools to airports) to be an attractive region for foreign investors and entrepreneurs.

All these factors and some others too, e.g. political stability, are essential in the tough 'Standortwettbewerb' (location competition) going on in the world and in Europe. Once again, it is necessary to perceive the competition for locations between communities and regions as well as the controversy, e.g. on 'Industriestandort Germany', as a result of insufficient effective demand resulting from the asymmetric adaptation mechanisms as imposed by the IMF and Maastricht Treaty. The 'Standortwettbewerb' between regions, as well as between nations, has for a long time been understood as zero or negative sum games.

The Money Factor in Metropolization and Peripherization

At present there are no signs of a tendency towards increased regional cooperation. On the contrary, increasing imbalances between the metropolitan areas and their peripheries can be observed. The outcome of 'Standortwettbewerb' is, as already mentioned, contributing to it. The establishment of a monetary union will strengthen the trend to a widening of existing gaps.

Basically, there are two factors at work: *First*, the Europe-wide competition within the banking sector will pave the way to a concentration process in which a number of international banks will gain in size and power at the expense of smaller and regionally based banks. Thereby, banking business will become more standardized with tailored services being restricted to big customers and investors, e.g. of one million EURO and more. The availability of loans to small firms in less developed regions that strongly rely on personal contacts and trust will tend to be reduced. This concentration process will impede the emergence and growth of new and small firms (Chick/Dow 1995, p.315) which generally are regarded as important bearers of innovation and structural change. This process is not apt to stimulate the development of peripheral regions. It may enforce the already known phenomenon of outflow of savings to the more attractive centres (Chick/Dow 1995, p.316).

Second, the establishment of a monetary union, by definition, puts an end to the national currencies and thereby eliminates a hitherto important policy instrument, namely, the exchange rate. Less-developed countries could thus reduce the cost pressure on their exports by devaluation (Herr 1995). This has proved to be a stimulating device even in the presence of higher interest rates, which devaluating countries usually have to pay for international credits and which they also have to offer to attract foreign investors.

Since within a currency union there are no exchange rates, what rules will have to be obeyed by debtor regions? The deficit resulting from outgoing payments (for imports) exceeding incoming revenues (for exports) can be closed (cf. Steindl 1989) by

(i)   dissaving,
(ii)   borrowing, and
(iii)   transfers (of agents active outside the region).

What happens, if (i) to (iii) are not sufficient to cover the deficit? Sales to the region will be reduced or regional firms unable to pay their debts will go bankrupt. That may induce foreign investors to take over the depreciated capital and start a new business. This would be a positive alternative. The negative one is a reduction of activities, or at least an impediment to development. A separate currency *would (presumably) provide* the option of reducing the export price by devaluating the currency.

To sum up: the present world monetary systems, the coming European one, with its asymmetric adaptation rules - as well as the ongoing concentration process in the European banking industry - will tend to increase already existing imbalances. It is doubtful, whether this process can be halted or reversed by monetary transfers, e.g., from the EU-funds. My scepticism is based not only on the size of the available funds, but also on the rules of the game.

My scepticism would also remain, if all Europe-wide infrastructural plans were to be implemented. For a prospering EU it is not sufficient to have competitive regions with competitive firms located in well functioning networks exchanging persons, commodities, services and information. In a waterway system, competitive ships and technically perfect waterways are not enough. To function, the system also needs sufficient water regulated by sufficient flood gates. What is needed in a *monetary system of regions*, in addition to all competitive qualities, is a sufficient supply of financial resources regulated by money gates. In the absence of it, some regions will tend to remain backward.

Widening the EU

The findings of sections 12,13 and 14 are particularly relevant in the context of a widening of the EU: the overriding economic challenge is the productivity and income gap between the EU and post-Communist countries. This issue merits closer scrutiny, and for this purpose the following diagrammatic analysis is offered.

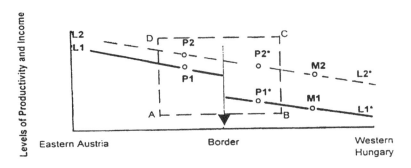

Figure 6.1 Transborder cooperation between poor and rich countries: The case of Eastern Austria and Western Hungary

Source: Author's own draft 1996

In the Figure 6.1, the L1L1* describes the decline of productivity/income from 'West to East', or from market-based to former centrally planned economies. Area ABCD is the region which is delineated for transborder cooperation. P1 is the 'rich', P1* the poor town. The slightly declining line L2L2* is the target of activities, namely, a great increase in the level of productivity/income in the 'Eastern' region, and a modest increase in the 'Western' one. The aim is to convert the towns P1 and P1*, separated by a border and an 'income-drop' into P2 and P2* with a similar level of productivity and income. The intention not to transfer the 'income-drop' eastward is equally important, i.e., to insure that town M1, located outside the transborder region ABCD, should parallelly increase its level of productivity/income from L1L1* to L2L2*.

A reduction of the productivity and income gap, and a gradual levelling out of the income slope is, in any case, a difficult task. It requires a profound change of the socio-economic contexts prevailing in the two regions. It would require a change of the four basic elements which constitute a socio-economic context:

1. The prevalent world views (including the 'mental maps'),
2. Its institutions, conventions and technologies as well as the interests and social practices expressing them,
3. The relative resource endowment (capital) as well as the relative costs, incomes, and prices,
4. The emanating and formative policies which influence 1 to 3.

We have suggested an AGENDA for the necessary change of the socio-economic contexts in the book called 'The Market Shock', which is now also available in Central and Eastern European languages. I refer you to this text for more details on the idea of context-making. I remain convinced that context-making is crucial for an improvement of transborder cooperation, as well as for the design of new institutions within the EU and within the global context, to change zero sum or negative sum games into positive sum games.

Staging of Cooperation

If the above analysis is sound, then the overriding objective for social science and social practice should be clear: it is to work for cooperative strategies, i.e. to elaborate the conditions of transforming zero and negative sum games into positive ones. This is certainly not an easy task.

At least three steps are needed to overcome the trend from positive to zero (negative) sum games. The first step amounts to making people aware of what is going on. It is crucial to introduce the idea of positive sum games into the mental maps of the relevant agents. You can only play a positive sum game by applying a cooperative strategy, if these are well marked in one's mental map.

The second step consists in designing positive sum games. If in the existing games the dominant (rational) strategy is non-cooperation, changes in the rules of the games have to be elaborated with the aim to make cooperation the dominating rational choice. It is a major scientific, as well as political, task to depict non-cooperative behaviour and processes in the regional development of Europe.

It would be a vital agenda to map those areas where private interests and the public European purpose diverge. Sections 12 and 13 can be considered as first indications for what ought to be the subject of ongoing scrutiny on which political decision can be based. If this is done, the staging of positive sum games can be approached in a third step. In this phase it is essential to gain the support of those agents upon whose cooperation or non-cooperation the outcome of the processes depend. This will only occur if the knowledge about costs and benefits of the games are well implemented in the minds of the players.

Research on the three steps recommends itself as a major research topic essential for a further development of European Spatial Development policies. It is best to be institutionalised as a network of research teams all over Europe and the European Union. It needs, however, to be coordinated from a small, efficient centre.

References

Chick, V./Dow, S., Wettbewerb und die Zukunft des europäischen Banken- und Finanzsystems". In: C. Thomasberger, ibid.

Georgescu-Roegen, N., *The Entropy Law and the Economic Process.* Harvard University Press 1971.

Herr, H., Die Europäische Währungsunion zwischen politischer Wünschbarkeit und ökonomischen Zwängen." In: C. Thomasberger, ibid.

Kregel, J.A., Matzner, E., Grabher, C., *The Market Shock.* Michigan University Press Ann Arbor 1992.

Matzner, E., Conclusions". In: Council of Europe (ed.), *Transborder Cooperation within sustainable regional/spatial planning in Central Europe.* European Regional Planning, No 55, 1993, pp.179-181.

Matzner, E., Instrument-Targeting or Context-Making? A New Look at the Theory of Economic Policy." *Journal of Economic Issues*, No. 2, June 1995.

Morgenstern, O., Thirteen Critical Points on Contemporary Economic Theory: An Interpretation." *Journal of Economic Literature*, Vol X, No 4, 1972.

Myrdal, G., *Economic Theory and Under-Developed Regions*. Duckworth, London 1957.

Robbins, L., *The Theory of Economic Policy of English Classical Political Economists*. Macmillan, London 1978 (1952).

Schelling, T.C., *Micromotives and Macrobehaviour*, Norton, New York 1978.

Soros, G., *Prospects for European Disintegration*. The SOROS Foundation, New York 1993.

Steindl, J., 'Diskussionsbeitrag zur EG-Frage", *Kursbuch*, Wien 1988, Na 3, p.3-7.

Thomasberger, C. (Hg.), *Europäische Geldpolitik zwischen Marktzwängen und neuen institutionellen Regelungen*. Metropolis, Marburg 1995.

Tinbergen, J., *Economic Policy: Principles and Design*. North Holland, Amsterdam 1959.

Tobin, J., Adjustment Responsibilities of Surplus and Deficit Countries." In: J. Tobin (ed.), *Essays in Economics, Theory and Policy*. MIT Press, Cambridge (USA) 1982.

Discussion by: Wolf Huber

I largely agree with E. MATZNER that
a)   The game theory is a fruitful approach to explain some basic features of decision-making processes;
b)   The prevalent 'rules of the game' do not support cooperative behaviour,
     and
c)   More cooperation would be desirable to avoid adverse social and economic effects of individual and group behaviour.

If we do not want to argue morally but want to come to a deeper scientific understanding, we cannot explain this lack of cooperative games by particular intellectual and/or moral deficiencies of political decision-makers. There must be - and indeed are - more serious limits to cooperative behaviour in policy-making which have to be taken into account if we look for possibilities to gradually improve cooperation at whatever political level:

1.   Real decision-making processes - particularly those in political life - are much more complex than models in game theory. There is usually a large number of players, each of which has a complex set of objectives. Each decision has not just one result (pay-off) but many, often interrelated, effects, and sometimes with considerable time-lags.
2.   Because of this complexity of reality there is a considerable amount of uncertainty about who are players, what their objectives and options are, and what would be the results of different actions. This uncertainty pertains also to the possibilities and possible effects of cooperation.
3.   As a further consequence of complexity and uncertainty, political players very often have (sets of) objectives which are inconsistent, 'fuzzy' and even contradicting each other. Therefore a decision can be 'cooperative' with regard to one objective and, at the same time, be 'non-cooperative' with regard to another objective.
4.   To reduce uncertainty and to deal with inconsistent and conflicting objectives, information processes (learning, negotiations etc.) are necessary which are much more time-consuming than generally believed. The very narrow limits of human capacity to process complex information within a given time are widely overlooked or underestimated in theories of planning and decision-making as well as in concepts of institutional reform of political and administrative structures.

Even if cooperative behaviour is regarded as a general value, these problems of complexity often make it necessary in practical decision-making to reduce complexity by -

a)   Cooperating only implicitly (by taking into account other interests, views, perspectives when taking a decision) but not explicitly (by exchanging information, negotiations etc.), or

b)   Choosing which of several conflicting objectives I want to cooperate with (and which not), or

c)   Taking an urgent decision without knowing all the possible effects on other interests (and thus taking the risk of maybe acting non-cooperatively).

PART III:
EVALUATION

7 Criteria for an Ex Ante Appraisal of Concepts of European Spatial Development Policies

PETER TREUNER [1]

Preliminary Remarks

The criteria of evaluation of 'European Spatial Development Policies' depend on the objectives to be pursued by such policies. The title suggested by the organisers of the workshop already suggests that there are different policy fields to be considered. In fact the interpretation of 'European Spatial Policies' concerns three fundamental issues.

Firstly, there are different interpretations of what is to be understood by 'Europe'. There is the 'Europe' of the European Union (now comprising 15 Member States), the much wider 'Europe' of the Council of Europe (now 39 member countries), and also the 'Europe' of the Organisation for Security and Cooperation in Europe (which is still limited to specific tasks in the vast realm of security aspects, and not yet a main partner in cooperation).

However, it must be kept in mind that, after the fall of the Iron Curtain and particularly after Russia was admitted to the Council of Europe - making Europe once more, after hundreds of years, a direct neighbour of China and other Asian countries - development objectives for the Union's spatial policies cannot be limited to the Union's Member States as such, but must at least consider the relations with its European neighbours outside the Union, and also the relations to the Union's neighbours in the Mediterranean Basin.

This underdeveloped aspect of European policies will not be dealt with in this contribution; it must suffice to indicate the urgency of renewing the Union's view of what is the European territory and its objective structure, to constitute the basis of rationally conceived spatial policies.[2]

Since the European Union, for the time being, is the only one of the three main 'Europes' that has set up policies and funds for achieving specific spatial objectives, the introduction will concentrate on aspects related to these policies.

Secondly, it must be seen that most of the fields in which the European Union has policy competence are, explicitly or implicitly, relevant for the Continent's spatial development. For the purpose of an introduction into the workshop's discussions it appears appropriate to concentrate on those fields of spatially relevant policies that were explicitly established with regard to spatial challenges, i.e. the Union's regional policy, its structural policy within the Common Agricultural Policy, and its more recent policy of developing Trans-European Communication Networks.

Thirdly, spatial structures can be considered at different spatial levels. Until now, there has been no consensus on the level of aggregation appropriate for concepts of European spatial policies. While the existing structural funds of the European Union are generally 'spatialised' to a level below the 'NUTS III' defined for statistical purposes, i.e. often down to the level of local (municipal) governments and administrations[3], this does not appear meaningful for a strategic approach to Europe's development, and is contradictory to the principle of subsidiarity now accepted by the European Union's members. The question of what would be meaningful spatial entities to analyse Europe's spatial structures and relations and to draw a spatial concept of development objectives cannot be discussed here, in spite of its fundamental importance.[4] However, I wish to point out that I start from the assumption that European spatial policies must be restricted to what cannot be achieved at the national and sub-national levels of government, and that Europe is too large and too differentiated to conceive a unique spatial approach for all parts of the Continent. There is the challenge to define 'macro-regions' within Europe, which will be aggregates of the regions defined by the European countries for their national planning purposes, and which most probably must be overlapping entities.[5]

Assumptions Concerning European Development Objectives

On the basis of the fundamental assumptions made explicit in the introductory remarks, I make the following assumptions which are necessary to approach the issue of evaluation criteria:
First: The strategic goal is

1. To create and strengthen the economic integration of Europe in the sense of establishing the missing links on 'Foucher's molecule'[6], to make economic interdependency strong enough to make conflicts too

costly for either partner, and thereby to create a basis for peace in Europe;

2. To give a special status to Russia with regard to its Asian dimension;
3. To make people and politicians accept, as a basis for operational policy decisions, that significant differences of living and development conditions will prevail in Europe for the next decades; and
4. To establish a minimum of European objectives of common and concerted spatial development, i.e. abandon the past approach of trying to add national objectives to each other and to replace this inefficient view by a transnational approach that concentrates on the Continent's crucial issues.

Second: The term 'European Spatial Development Policies' refers first of all, although not exclusively, to the European Union's structural funds which must be reconsidered and reshaped within a few years with the objective and under the constraint of optimising the European-wide effects of limited transferable resources.

Third: The basic institutional framework (European Union / Council of Europe / Organisation for Security and Cooperation in Europe) will not be questioned and changed in a fundamental way by the modifications of the European treaties to be discussed and prepared by the Inter-Governmental Conference ('Maastricht II').

Fourth: Peace must and will be established on the Balkans.

It is furthermore assumed that the term 'development policy' stands for the idea to improve the pattern of changes with regard to the strategic objectives, by re-allocating resources to meet priority requirements or needs.

Finally, it is assumed that evaluation is understood as the ex ante appraisal of feasible operational action programmes, carried out by 'experts' to the best of their knowledge, to serve as a basis for policy decisions, i.e. not by 'politicians' (in governments or parliaments) who face the struggle for political legitimation. It is assumed that subsequent policy decisions will be the closer to the experts' concepts the more convincingly these have been elaborated.

It must be accepted that these assumptions can all be questioned, and that there is no guarantee that they will hold true. However, without such a set of basic assumptions, no strategic approach can be rationally evaluated. In the given situation, which is characterized by many fundamental uncertainties - e.g. regarding the future role of Russia, pcacc on the Balkans, the continuation of Western Europe's readiness to conceive and implement solidarity as a key instrument to maintain and stabilize peace -

any approach to a somewhat rational evaluation must take uncertain, speculative decisions on such basic options.

Criteria for the Ex Ante Appraisal of Concepts of 'European Spatial Development Policies'

In this presentation, orientated towards necessary political decisions, the term 'criteria' is used for checks designed to find out whether a policy concept is good enough to be recommended to policy makers, and possibly to be accepted by them.

In the following, only the seven criteria which appear to be the most fundamental ones will be briefly presented.

Ability to Respond to European (i. e. Non-National) Priorities

The European Community's past 'juste retour' approach, which, in spite of some laudable efforts to overcome it, is still predominant, must be replaced by a new view that is governed by long- term needs of stability and development conditions.

The border regions approach is a particularly suitable example for the necessary change of approach. While today virtually all border regions (within the Union) can profit from European support programmes, future border programmes must be conceived and implemented to care for those specific border problems of European significance which cannot be overcome by the concerned neighbour states alone.[7]

Respect of the Principle of Subsidiarity

It must be understood - and translated into political decisions - that the principle of subsidiarity is not merely a philosophical idea of some intellectual attractiveness but a crucial condition for maintaining Europe's greatest treasure and strength, i.e. its diversity. European programmes and activities that simply substitute for the inability of national and sub-national governments, do not correspond to the principle of subsidiarity. It must be accepted that - within reasonable limits - individual and even contradictory development policy approaches can be followed by national governments in Europe; but it must also become accepted that at the European level decisions must be governed by Europe-wide considerations, and corresponding priorities. Today's programmes are somewhat closer to this concept than they were ten or twenty years ago - but they are still far away from being characterized by such a trans-national view.

Minimum of Compatible Analytical Foundations

Development concepts and corresponding spatial development policies require analytical foundations that are based on internationally and inter-regionally compatible information concepts which provide that similar phenomena become recognisable in similar forms.

Balance Between Efficiency and Integration

The fundamental dilemma characterized by efficiency-orientation, on the one hand, and welfare or integration-orientation, on the other, must be accepted and solved in a pragmatic way, defining the relative priority given to either one. With regard to development perspectives in a wider Europe this decision will have more serious implications as in the past of a small community of economically more homogeneous member countries. The fundamental question requiring an operational answer is whether a unique approach can be maintained, pretending to pursue the same welfare and integration objectives for all of the Union's territories, or whether a Europe of two or even three 'speeds' offers a more realistic perspective. The present discussions of how to establish a monetary union ('single currency') indicates the options to be discussed and decided with regard to the Union's future spatial policy approach. The political dimension of such discussions and decisions will have to be considered. Spatial policy proposals must take into account this aspect and contain clear views of the objective followed.

Relation Between Short-Term and Long-Term Development Objectives

Another fundamental question concerns the time horizon of future spatial policy decisions. Although it appears simple and reasonable to propose a twofold approach which conceives short-term policies within a framework of long-term objectives and the elaboration of policy approaches for the immediate future of the next five or ten years, decision-makers may be well advised to concentrate on the short-term approach. At the same time the long-term framework should be reduced to a minimum of long-term priorities which are likely to constitute elements of more detailed long-term views. These may become meaningful after a transition period of a decade or so. The few elements of long-term tasks included in the map already referred to[8] may serve as an example for such a reduced approach which remains open to include additional elements when clearer perspectives of Europe's future structure become visible.

Programme Character of Policies

So far spatial policy concepts are still characterized by a sector approach, in spite of the increased efforts of inter-fund coordination. The evaluation of the next generation of policy approaches must be further developed in accordance with the line of approach of the last reform of the structural funds; i.e., giving a still greater importance to the complementary nature of actions in the different policy fields; to be put together in multi-dimensional programmes orientated towards pragmatically defined common spatial development objectives and within the framework of a minimum of long-term goals. Isolated projects, as in the present approach to support trans-national networks, could be advocated as a first step into a new field of Community actions, but must be integrated, in the future, into more comprehensive programmes of spatial development.

Partnership Approach

Finally it is important to conceive future spatial policy approaches in a more partnership- orientated way, making the cooperation of local and regional governments, other institutions, enterprises and citizens a basic element of programme formulation and implementation.

Other Aspects of Spatial Policy Evaluation

Of course, there are other crucial aspects - e.g. the various time horizons of integration to be considered, assumptions concerning the financial and the institutional feasibility (constraints) of European integration and, last but not least, the philosophical origins and justifications of spatial development objectives - that would also merit some thought and will require careful consideration in the long run. These aspects could not be touched upon within the framework of this workshop.

A Short (and Superficial) Screening of Actual European Spatial Policy

If we take a brief, and admittedly too superficial, look at the existing European Regional Development Fund as the most interesting example of explicitly space-orientated Community policy, we must first of all underline its impressive evolution from an instrument used for refunding national regional development policies to a much more independent instrument of European importance, in order to avoid total misunderstanding. However, with regard to the seven main objectives outlined in the preceding section, the state of affairs is not too convincing:

The first objective - to respond to European priorities (i. e. not to a sum of national priorities) - could not in the past, and still now cannot be achieved simply because there is no such view of what European spatial development priorities are. Hence the elaboration of such objectives, as presently attempted by the Spatial Development Committee of the Union's Member States[9], must be regarded as a particularly important approach to improve European spatial policies.

The second objective - to respect the principle of subsidiarity - still remains an abstract category. The fact that the Union's organs wish to remain master of the Union's funds, on the one hand, and that all those local, regional and sometimes national governments expect financial and sometimes institutional and political relief from the various programmes offered, on the other hand, has as a result that decisions at the European level remain predominant. This is true, for example, for many of the activities under the INTERREG programmes which support activities that mostly are meaningful, but which could as well be prepared and executed by the partners concerned on either side of the border in question.

The third objective - to prepare and conceive spatial development programmes on the basis of a minimum of compatible analytical foundations - also remains unfulfilled, due to the incompatibility of most of the regionalized information available under the present system of spatial units (NUTS nomenclature) utilised by EUROSTAT.

The fourth objective - to lay open and to justify the relative priorities attached to efficiency and to integration objectives - is not achieved at all, in spite of considerations of such type that are certainly underlying the present programmes, but which are not justified in any 'objective' way.

The fifth objective - to lay open the relative importance given to short-term versus long-term development objectives - is also not fulfilled in the present programmes in such a way that the reasons can be recognised and compared with other cases.

The sixth objective - to coordinate the activities of various policy programmes with each other and with ongoing and additional development activities of the national and sub-national governments concerned - has found much more recognition and attention in the present generation of structural fund programmes. The fact that such approaches to improve inter-programme coordination remain unsatisfactory results mainly from the absence of fundamental conditions such as a long-term view of spatial development priorities and of a minimum of inter-regionally comparable analytical foundations.

The seventh objective - to give a key role to partnership approaches - has become popular and widely accepted during the past few years. However, its application contradicts somewhat the objective of strengthening the application of the principle of subsidiarity, since the role of the Union's participation tends to favour a case by case approach, thereby undermining the Union's responsibility for programmes responding to defined European priorities.

This short evaluation of the present state of affairs appears to be quite unsatisfactory. It must be kept in mind, however, that the Community's and nowadays the Union's attempts to establish and to manage important funds could not start from any comparable experience, and that tremendous progress has been achieved with regard to the beginnings of the fund policies three decades ago. It can be hoped, and must be hoped in the interest of stabilising the Union as the only conceivable motor of European integration, that more and faster progress will be made in our present phase of European transition. Spatial development researchers have been called upon to contribute, not merely by descriptive and analytical contributions, but also by taking an active part in the discussion on feasible ways out of the still unsatisfactory present state of European spatial policies.

Notes

1   A summary of an oral contribution to *The Vienna Workshop*.

2   Cf. Peter Treuner, Michel Foucher: Towards a New European Space. Akademie für Raumforschung und Landesplanung: Hannover 1995.

3   Cf. European Commission, Europe 2000+, Cooperation for European territorial development, Luxembourg 1994, p.24. - Cf. Map 3 Regions eligible for Community regional assistance, from 1994. In: European Commission, Europe 2000+, Cooperation for European territorial development, Luxembourg 1994, p.28.

4   Cf. Peter Treuner, Institutional and Instrumental Aspects of a New European Regionalized Development Strategy. In: Peter Treuner, Michel Foucher, op.cit., pp. 80-85.

5   Cf. the most interesting presentation of existing European regional associations in: European Commission, Europe 2000+, Cooperation for European territorial development, Luxembourg 1994, p.24. - Cf. also the schematic aggregation of European macro-regions proposed by Bruno Amoroso in Peter Treuner, Michel Foucher, op.cit., (Figure No. 2).

6   Cf. Michel Foucher: Fragments d'Europe, Paris 1993, p. 281.

7   Cf Peter Treuner, Michel Foucher: New European Challenges. In: Peter Treuner, Michel Foucher, op.cit., p. 6-18, and also Map 2.

8   Cf. Peter Treuner, Michel Foucher, op.cit., Map 1.

9   European Spatial Planning.Results of the Informal Council of Spatial Planning Ministers, Leipzig, 21/22 September 1994.

Discussion by: Elisabeth Holzinger

My approach to evaluation is a theoretical one. From a political scientist's point of view, I consider evaluation as a political tool as well as a policy in itself. Therefore, you have to take into account the preconditions for your subject, in this case regional policy, and declare the special aim you have using evaluation in the political process.

In my short presentation I will focus on five issues formulated as a hypothesis, while being aware of the fact that a hypothesis always involves some degree of exaggeration.

Our subject is uncertainty

This uncertainty is caused by the characteristics of spatial and regional development policy. Let me list just a few of these characteristics:

1. Spatial and regional development includes various and different policy areas; therfore a cooperative network should work, but unfortunately does not always exist;
2. As a social pattern, spatial and regional development policy is affected by contradictory interests, motivations and responsibilities which lead to deviations;
3. In such a heterogenous field conflicts between goals do, of course, exist - but a lot of preliminary work should have been done to foster harmony;
4. By causing certain effects the preconditions of your policy change so you never know exactly whether you satisfy the right needs;
5. And a final characteristic is that, as a consequence, the uncertainty about the relations between goals and means in this field is particularly high.

Therefore, it is all the more important to find adequate models to act rationally under these conditions. In my opinion EVA can support you.

Nevertheless, policy should be able to answer the simple question: What use has it?

Policy should be evaluable because there is a lack of AND a duty to accountability in the public sector. That does not mean introducing rigorous controls going around with a yardstick and looking around like blind mice for effects.

For me, as a social scientist who considers policy as a social pattern, it is clear that you have to find ways and means to handle a matter that, as it becomes effective, is currently and constantly changing its initial conditions; ways and means to understand the course of actions, i.e., what is going on while implementing policy, and ways and means to recognize the effects of intervention.

This is an ambitious task, and leads to my third issue:

Under volatile and uncertain circumstances, the simple question does not receive a simple answer

I do not know if you agree that our subject is uncertainty. Anyway, let me first stress that there is a strong connection between how you consider your subject and how you practise evaluation. Reflecting on EVA and selecting one EVA philosophy implies simultaneous reflection on planning and policy-making while following one planning philosophy.

One approach to planning is a technocratic one. It believes in linearity when identifying problems - goal-setting - implementation - effects - feed-back and when starting again.

This approach corresponds to an EVA-model in which such a linear sequence of events exists and every step of this logical framework can be evaluated. Its main focus is on effects and efficiency, assuming that these can be found, measured and evaluated.

There is another approach to planning and policy-making:

1. Not simple, but adequate for handling uncertainty and complexity:
2. Starting from some guidelines, differentiate them by regional adjustment together with regional and local actors;
3. Then really operationalize goals by discussing them, and avoid master plans with heroic and unattainable goals;
4. Consider the multiple interests and contradictory goals of the administrative agencies at the different levels of administration;
5. Build a network of cooperation among partners.

This approach needs **another EVA concept**, which means implementing EVA as an interactive learning process. Its focus is on the way of acting; to understand the barriers for acting you have to work with the stakeholders. All in all, this means learning by doing and the establishing of structures where possible.

There are at least 6 preconditions for an EVA based on learning

If EVA serves as a necessary instrument for reflection, i.e., a tool setting in motion a learning process within the system of political-administration, there are some prerequisites:

1. INTEGRATION of EVA within the policy-making and planning processes;
2. ACCEPTANCE of EVA;
3. ORGANIZATIONAL STRUCTURES where the discussion could take place;
4. TRANSPARENCY regarding the tasks, functions and roles of evaluators, as well as the decision which EVA-results should be available and to whom;
5. PARTICIPATION of stakeholders;
6. TO BE READY FOR INNOVATION - you have to be aware that you are participating in an experiment.

What are the main tasks EVA projects should deal with?

As I see it

1. Learning about EVA itself: that means watching the progess made in implementing an evaluation culture in Austria;
2. Learning about policy-making - that means policy evaluation in order to understand the transition of goals into action;
3. Analysing how spatial and regional development policy can contribute to achieve labour market effects;
4. Discovering structural effects can be caused by integrating the Eastern countries.

One final remark

In Austria, a country with less limited experience in EVA in the field of spatial planning and regional policy, we have to decide right now about our EVA-strategy, the concept we want to follow, and how we can establish a common understanding.

To set this process in motion, the EU's structural policy was, and is, an important factor - but for me this is not a priority.

There are special rules for evaluation issued by the EU which we have to observe. However, a critical reception of the EU's evaluation concept is also necessary, as well as the development of an adjusted Austrian way of carrying this out.

Thank you for the opportunity to address you.

PART IV: CONCLUSIONS

8 European Spatial Policies as a Political Requirement

FRIEDRICH SCHINDEGGER

The opening up of a new political level of activity for spatial planning began only a few years ago. Therefore European spatial development policy is new - not only for Austria. What is important for our considerations is that, until now, this level has not been clearly defined regarding institutional and instrumental aspects, but is itself rather the subject of a development process.

An interesting point in this context is the story of how spatial development policy on the European level came into operation. It was not brought about because it has been a task imposed on it by constitution, which would have agreed with the tradition of most Member States. It rather grew out of a political need that developed from a situation which is distinguished by

· The strong expansion and intensification of EU regional policies through the EU's Structure Funds with their programme orientation;

· The spatial impact of the EU's uncoordinated sector policies;

· And finally the new responsibilities of the Maastricht Treaty regarding the Community's measures with spatial impact on environmental and trans-European Networks which include enlargening the financing instruments of the EU.

Thus, one could say that the European Community, at that time, was forced by the matter itself to introduce the coordination of its policies supported by planning. I am talking about this genesis of a purpose-oriented development of the instrument, because later on another perspective obviously became topical, and this was influenced more by the classical concept of comprehensive spatial planning.

The original approach seems to me to be represented by the first document of the Commission 1991: *Europe 2000: Outlook for the development of the Community's territory.*

This document was not conceived as an overall plan but rather as a strategic guide.

Thus it does not draft any final structural model for Europe in the future, but rather shows the development trends of those factors crucial for spatial development, and from which conclusions on the problems and opportunities in the individual regions are reached.

In an intentional opposition, the project *European Spatial Development Perspective (E.S.D.P.)* represents the so-called classical comprehensive approach (I call it a project because there is still no draft in sight).

The answer to policy challenge should not be *geo-design* but guidance for sector policy measures

From my point of view, a master-plan philosophy does make sense on the local level and to some degree on the regional level, but it makes hardly any sense on the national level and still less on the European level. As far as the national or European level is concerned, the classical, comprehensive, planning approach lacks political relevance, because there is in fact no adequate, comprehensive, policy responsibility. This principal failure of the approach cannot be corrected by associating it with the claim for more competence for comprehensive planning on central government levels. On these levels policy is usually implemented and also designed only in sector terms - and I think there are good reasonsfor this.

Therefore, from my point of view, it is the task of spatial planning (and research) on the European level to analyse what the spatial effects are - for example, of common agricultural policy or EU transport policy - and then to give guidelines for a regional differentiation of such sector policies to meet the general goal of cohesion by regional adjustment. Very first steps to that approach can be recognized in the CAP with regard to the mountain areas and may be soon even in transport policy (as may be expected according to a recent statement made by Commissioner Neil Kinnock).

I think that spatial planning should not repeat on the European level what was happening in the past on lower levels. It should

1. Keep to general objectives and ideal models of final structures;
2. Not transform its own goals into the categories of sector policy;
3. And thus rely on automatic implementation by sector policy measures.

The experience on regional and national levels has shown, that the expectations of spatial planning cannot be achieved in this manner. Nowhere have spatial planning concepts guided the development, for example, of national urban systems. In most cases, those plans are a mysterious mix of ex-post interpretations and future design elements without policy reference. My conclusion is that we do not need *geo-design*, but strategic guidelines for spatially differentiated action - and action is always happening in the field of certain sector policies.

What we really need are territorially defined standards in terms of economic performance, labour market situation, access to trans-European Networks etc. These standards have to refer to the living conditions of the population concerned as well as to the demands for the public actors concerned and they have to make policy programmes, efforts and achievements measurable and evaluable from a territorial point of view. In my opinion these are the requirements spatial development planning conceptions have to meet, and in particular, on the European level.

The main task in the central European EU-periphery is cohesion - this side and beyond the external border of the EU - also on the national level

Let me now focus your attention on the main issue of our region, which is at the same time Central European and EU-periphery. Let me say it in the words of the Commission: I would like to quote their second document: *Europe 2000+ Cooperation for European territorial development*: 'Community regions with common borders with Central and Eastern European Countries, which were previously places of confrontation, are now undergoing the greatest change. However, they face a range of problems:

1. Major differences in income between the two sides of the border which are a threat to stability (in the form of illegal immigration and massive relocation of companies in particular);
2. Differences in institutions and political culture which often impede the development of cooperation;
3. Differences in infrastructure which require border regions to have a special place in European network policy'.

'The more integrated the Union becomes, the more the border effect threatens to be an issue in peripheral areas, possibly heightening their sense of isolation. Nevertheless, because of their location, external border regions have the capability of developing closer relations with other countries and cultures ....' *(end of citation)*

Even in the most favourable scenario of development, the clear disparities in prices and wages at that border will remain for a long time. The probability of achieving a relatively balanced situation comparable to Austria's western borders within this period of time is very low. Austria has the advantage of being a direct neighbour to the countries in the process of reform with the comparatively best outlook for development. In spite of this, Austria's borders to the East show how wide the gap at the eastern periphery of western Europe could be.

In the long run, no exact demarcation lying precisely 50 km east of Vienna and dividing prosperous regions will exist. What will evolve is a zone with differing levels of prosperity which are overlapping the borders from both sides. The disparities between and within the countries of eastern Europe in the process of reform will be contiguous to the disparities within the EU. Therefore special care should be given to matters of spatial policy in that region.

Let me draw your attention again to the so called *Lackó-slope*, which was mentioned yesterday. Any tilting of that slope would produce considerable internal political problems in the countries affected by growing regional disparities within a national perspective. The steeper the slope, the stronger political resistance against cross border cooperation will occur; in other words, a loss of national cohesion and thus an obstacle against lifting up the slope at all. That shows again the importance of a distinguished regional policy in that area.

Regional policy on the EU's external border has to be shaped with participation of the cities as the regional centres

First of all, regional policy on the EU's external borders and beyond these should, in my opinion, reach further than the perspectives have done until now, as these have only perceived assisted areas and subsidy funds. From a spatial planning policy point of view, the fixation on the EU's structure fund *objective areas* seems to me to be disastrous and to lead to the situation, in which large urban areas in Austria once again become 'white spots' in the *mental maps* of the regional policy-makers. Cities and urban regions have not played a role in Austria's regional policies until now; neither actively nor passively. Urban policy does not exist at all in Austria.

There is a threat that the practice prevailing until now will continue: Federal and State governments have, once again, an eye only for economically weak areas - now under the EU label *Objective 1, 2 and 5b areas* - and the municipalities of the large urban areas carry out, more or less, their own location policies, usually in competition with the urban hinterlands or vice versa.

Nobody feels responsible for the intelligent use of the potentials of the 'locomotives' of regional development, the real regional centres on a European scale. This is contrasted by the concept underlying the document *Europe 2000+*. It practically promotes the specific development of medium-sized cities (those are our large cities) and the creation of networks between medium and small sized cities. In my opinion, Austria should receive particular attention, in view of the high demands and its difficult starting situation at the eastern border of the EU.

Regional policy at the EU's external borders and beyond these means that regional development policies have to take into account the conditions and development trends in the corresponding regions beyond the border. In my opinion, cities must become active as regional centres, here as in any other kind of region. Particularly at the external border this cannot be left to the bordering municipalities alone.

Based on location conditions and historic links, there seem to be rather good conditions for cross-border co-operation between Austrian cities and regional centres in the neighbouring countries. Areas of co-operation could be the expansion of the cross-border regional transportation and telecommunications networks, cross-border media centres, common cultural projects and educational programmes, enterprise interlinking, municipal economies and tourism marketing, among others. The EU has developed special instruments for that kind of cooperation.

To develop a EU-centre for Central and Eastern Europe

The EU is confronted with quite a new challenge. The process between promoting integration across the eastern borders and extending the territory to Central Europe, can be compared to a walking tour on a narrow ridge. One of the necessary answers should be a EU-authority of its own which is responsible for the relations to the associated partners and future members in the eastern part of Central Europe. It is quite obvious that this type of institution should deal especially with regional development. Finally, I would like to name some of the tasks of such an institution from my point of view, and with regard to the three dimensions we have discussed here.

Within the framework of the Structure Funds **evaluation** is just now becoming a systematic element of programme planning. Besides this level of programme evaluation, as much attention should be given on a more aggregated level to the shape of the whole conception of that kind of spatial policy. It should be based on the above mentioned territorial standards for living conditions and public activities, particularly concerning the regional policy beyond the EU-borders in wider Europe or in the context of widening the EU.

Considering the fast-growing number of such programme evaluations, a systematic exchange of experience in methodology as well as in the way evaluations are executed is necessary. The MEANS-programme delivered first insights in evaluation theory and practice. In order to achieve a more common standard, a scientific network should be established. On the other hand, evaluation by spatial policy objectives is also necessary for other EU-policy sectors with important impacts on the spatial development, as for example CAP and transport policy. In terms of budget expenditure these policy fields seem to deserve much more attention by regional research and spatial planning. Again this is of relevance for any kind of programme-based expenditures with spatial implications of the EU in Central and Eastern European countries too.

The complexity and dynamics of the economic-political development requires an intensive discussion of different possible spatial developments in the context of different political conditions. **Prospective scenarios** of the future development of spatial structures in a wider Europe need the integration of serious efforts of different kinds of scientists and planners, in order to summarize plausible assumptions on trends and intervention strategies in a consistent model.

Conventional approaches are not very helpful. The completely new challenge of the transformation and integration of Central and Eastern Europe without any historic example does not allow classical empiric approaches. General visions, which try to put the whole spatial system in a totalitarian manner into one picture, are not really helpful. In order to define appropriate subjects of the prospective scenarios, the two documents *Europe 2000* and *Europe 2000+* could give some orientation. Based on 'strategic analysis' they try to deal with prospective changes in the areas of demography, migration, industrial location, transport, infrastructure etc. on the one hand, and in certain types of spatial structures such as urban areas, rural areas, border areas, etc., on the other hand.

Essential for this type of interdisciplinary work is the continuity, which should be guaranteed by an independent institution responsible for the 'production' of planning materials as a basis for the multilateral dialogue between Member States, associated countries and the Commission.

A purely collective or multilateral approach in the planning production, in my opinion, does not work. The experiences made within countries organised as federations ought to teach us that the price to be paid for this type of collective responsibility - in the best of cases - is a high degree of abstraction and the lack of content in the statements. From my point of view, it would be too much to expect Member States to develop a sufficiently concrete political programme collectively. For this reason, for example, State programmes are not elaborated on by conferences of the municipalities, but the municipalities do have the opportunity to state their positions on matters in an endorsement procedure.

There is a connection with the principle of subsidiarity. To follow that principle, in my opinion, means that competence for tasks should be distributed according to the capability of the corresponding levels. Each level has its own particular specific policy responsibility and functional capacity. If competence is wrongly appointed, from below, then the result is unjustifiable hegemony; or, if from above, overstraining.

The lesson to be learned arising from the horizontal cross-border cooperation of regions and States, as well as the vertical cooperation between the Commission, Member States, regions and local authorities, is that the development of **cooperation strategies** has to be seen as a task for scientific and planning work in its own right.

The enormous diversity of political-administrative structures is part of the diversity of political cultures - as it comes out very well in the project of the Commission named *Compendium*, which deals with a description and analysis of the *Spatial Planning Systems* of the member countries. And thinking about cooperation strategies, one has to take into account this variety of political culture, of which planning systems are a central issue. Therefore the variety of planning systems has to be accepted as a basic condition for spatial planning on the European level. In this context we have to recognize that, for example, the new-born States of Central and Eastern Europe conceive the development of systems of their own which are different to those of their former partners as part of their identity achievement. So there is a large area of tasks for professional work. A start has to be made by explaining the systems to each other - as the above mentioned *Compendium* endeavours - to gain, first of all, an understanding of the differences and then, on that basis, an analysis of the possibilities of certain cooperation strategies using the know-how of operations research and related sciences.

From my point of view, neither unification of planning systems nor the introduction of a central executive competence for comprehensive planning on the European level are appropriate concepts with respect to the political diversity of European countries and the needs of political planning. I am convinced that cooperation in that context can operate only within the concept of networking. This again, it seems to me, is a call for an institution of its own for continuous professional monitoring, information exchange, evaluation etc. This new institution would have to function as a kind of infrastructure for the development of cooperation.

In a public meeting of the Austrian Conference on Regional Planning in January 1995, I made a recommendation that the Austrian government should promote the concept of such a new institution within the EU, and that the City of **Vienna should apply for candidature**. There are already a considerable number of appropriate research and scientific institutions that could serve as a base in Vienna. The know-how of already established national and international institutions which could become, or already are, active in this field is a fact that should not be underestimated.

By the way, this is a good example of how spatial planning policy sometimes - and this applies to the European level even more than to the national level - may be implemented beyond the usual categories of zoning, infrastructure and protected areas. Foreign policy, science and research policy and regional policy combined into one concrete project seem to me to be a very effective spatial planning strategy on the European level.

Half a year ago Mr. Hannes Swoboda, the responsible member of the city government of Vienna, announced that the Commission is providing an *Institute for technical aid and information exchange for the preparation of the eastern extension of the EU* to be located in Vienna. Maybe this is already the first step towards confirming this idea.

Index

—A—

additionality 81
Agricultural 42; 134
air transport 38
area 12; 17; 30; 71; 81; 88; 120; 121;
   152; 155
Austria 11; 32; 58; 79; 80; 81; 82; 101;
   105; 109; 111; 125; 144; 149; 152;
   153

—B—

Belgium 31; 32; 75; 95
Blue Banana 13; 15
budget 37; 42; 154

—C—

CAP 150; 154
Capital 27; 93
Central 2; 3; 5; 13; 39; 41; 48; 87; 91;
   95; 126; 151; 153; 154; 155
central Europe 151
Commission 2; 10; 12; 17; 27; 28; 37;
   42; 43; 80; 86; 89; 91; 92; 93; 95; 97;
   149; 151; 154; 155; 156
Committee of the Regions 1; 11; 15; 17;
   97
Common 134
Community 10; 79; 86; 87; 89; 91; 92;
   136; 138; 139; 140; 149; 151
Council 1; 10; 11; 20; 27; 28; 79; 97;
   133; 135
Council of Europe 11; 27; 133; 135
Council of Ministers 28
County 30
Czech Republic 48

—D—

Denmark 35; 95
Development 1; 2; 5; 9; 10; 11; 15; 27;
   28; 29; 39; 43; 50; 85; 86; 89; 93; 97;
   100; 126; 133; 135; 136; 137; 138;
   139; 150

District 15

—E—

EC 84; 86; 87
Ecological 13; 14
employment 14; 34; 51; 70; 81; 84; 88;
   89; 91; 96; 105; 107; 117; 120; 121
English 119
enlargement 24; 37; 48; 102
Environmental 15
European 1; 2; 3; 4; 5; 9; 10; 11; 12; 13;
   14; 15; 16; 17; 18; 20; 22; 23; 24; 27;
   28; 29; 30; 31; 32; 33; 34; 35; 36; 37;
   38; 40; 41; 42; 43; 44; 45; 46; 47; 48;
   49; 50; 51; 53; 57; 58; 59; 60; 61; 62;
   66; 68; 70; 71; 72; 73; 74; 75; 79; 80;
   82; 83; 84; 86; 87; 89; 91; 92; 93; 94;
   95; 96; 97; 99; 100; 120; 124; 126;
   133; 134; 135; 136; 137; 139; 140;
   141; 149; 150; 151; 153; 154; 155;
   156
European Commission 2; 10; 12; 17;
   27; 28; 37; 80; 89
European integration 24; 35; 120; 139;
   141
European Parliament 1; 42; 62; 79; 97
European Spatial Development Perspective 9; 11; 15; 150

—F—

Finland 79
France 31; 32; 38; 41; 95

—G—

Germany 16; 17; 30; 31; 32; 34; 41; 95;
   96; 122
Greece 96

—H—

Housing 41
Hungary 48; 125

—I—

Industrial 59; 64; 68; 71; 105
infrastructure 23; 30; 33; 38; 51; 81; 85;
   86; 89; 90; 91; 92; 99; 111; 122; 151;
   154; 156
Integration 24; 40; 137
investment 15; 38; 39; 40; 42; 43; 51;
   80; 81; 82; 83; 84; 85; 94; 95; 96; 97;
   103
Ireland 89; 96
Italy 34; 95

—L—

Land 36
land use 31; 42; 45
Limits 83; 86
loan 94; 96
Local 49; 60; 65; 66; 67; 68; 71; 72; 75;
   97
location 14; 29; 31; 33; 38; 86; 87; 102;
   103; 108; 122; 151; 153; 154

—M—

Maastricht 10; 12; 23; 38; 58; 59; 60;
   72; 79; 94; 97; 120; 122; 135; 149
Monetary 12; 121

—N—

National 34; 35; 70; 86; 136
Netherlands 95
networking 4; 17; 85; 86; 87; 89; 90;
   91; 92; 93; 96; 97; 99; 100; 112; 155

—P—

Payment 121
Planning 1; 2; 10; 12; 91; 155; 156
Poland 15; 48
Policy 1; 2; 60; 64; 68; 69; 71; 83; 84;
   86; 87; 93; 134; 139; 142
Political 61; 66
Portugal 22; 96
Public 65; 67

—R—

Red Octopus 2; 9; 13; 14; 15; 18
Regional 1; 2; 5; 10; 41; 62; 83; 85; 86;
   87; 92; 93; 95; 97; 105; 113; 122;
   139; 152; 153; 156
regional development 30; 61; 69; 81;
   82; 83; 92; 100; 122; 126; 139; 142;
   144; 153
regional policy 5; 23; 37; 51; 60; 61;
   62; 63; 64; 66; 67; 68; 69; 73; 74; 79;
   81; 96; 100; 134; 142; 144; 152; 154;
   156
regulations 49; 80
Rural 33
Russia 133; 135; 136

—S—

Schools 92
service 31; 38; 66; 81; 105
single currency 94; 120; 137
single market 22; 88
Slovakia 48
social 10; 22; 23; 33; 36; 37; 41; 44; 51;
   60; 61; 63; 71; 82; 85; 89; 92; 101;
   104; 117; 118; 120; 122; 125; 126;
   128; 142
Spain 95; 96
State 12; 35; 37; 58; 59; 60; 63; 64; 65;
   66; 67; 68; 69; 70; 71; 73; 74; 75; 84;
   152; 155
Strategic 86; 87; 118
structural funds 80; 81; 134; 135; 138
Structure 1; 13; 14; 149; 153
subsidiarity 4; 79; 100; 134; 137; 139;
   140; 155
Subsidies 86
sustainability 24; 47
Sustainable 47
Sweden 60; 61; 62; 67; 68; 69; 70; 71;
   73; 74; 82
Switzerland 35

—T—

telecommunication 16; 39; 40; 45; 97
Tourism 81
transport policy 150; 154

—U—

UK 88; 89; 95
University 79
Urban 13; 32; 36; 41; 152
USA 42

USSR 10

—V—

Visegrad 48

For Product Safety Concerns and Information please contact our EU
representative GPSR@taylorandfrancis.com Taylor & Francis Verlag GmbH,
Kaufingerstraße 24, 80331 München, Germany

Printed and bound by CPI Group (UK) Ltd, Croydon, CR0 4YY
08/05/2025
01864412-0003